The Actor's Choice

The Actor's Choice

The Transition from Stage to Screen

Thomas W. Babson

HEINEMANN
Portsmouth, NH

Heinemann
A division of Reed Elsevier Inc.
361 Hanover Street
Portsmouth, NH 03801-3912

Offices and agents throughout the world

The author and publisher wish to thank Paramount Studios and Ted Danson, John Ratzenberger, Rhea Perlman, and George Wendt for generously giving permission to reprint the photographs appearing on pp. 112–15.

Library of Congress Cataloging-in-Publication Data

Babson, Thomas W.
    The actor's choice : the transition from stage to screen / Thomas W. Babson
        p.   cm.
    ISBN 0-435-07009-6
    1. Motion picture acting. 2. Acting for television. I. Title.
PN1995.9.A26B23   1996
791.43'028—dc20   96-4350
                                                                CIP

Editor: Lisa A. Barnett
Production: Vicki Kasabian
Cover design: Jenny Jensen Greenleaf

Printed in the United States of America on acid-free paper
99 98 97 96   DA   1 2 3 4 5

Contents

Foreword

*T*his is my first foreword, but I wish it were my second foreword so I would have some idea of what to say in my first. I also wish it were spelled "four-word" because then I would already be done.

An actor trying to make the leap from stage to screen can learn techniques for doing so by reading this book. It wonderfully details the ways to narrow that gap. But an actor must also bring something to the dance that no book can teach him—truth and humanity, which transcend the gap between the image and the audience. The actor needs to feel so that the audience can feel. The stage actor will do well to study the chapters here and listen to Tom, because he has made the jump successfully. We are all lucky that he chose to go back and impart what he learned to others.

Thomas Babson played "Tom Babson" on *Cheers*. (We dropped the *h* so he could use if for "humanity.") Cliff may have made fun of him because he couldn't pass the bar; but this book underscores the truth of his most famous line: "Tom Babson undefeated."

— *James Burrows*

Acknowledgments

I wrote a play when I was in graduate school called *Eternity Street* that dealt with an individual's decisions made over the course of a lifetime. The premise was that decisions, no matter how important or urgently made, were decided as the result of a lifetime of experience and learning from the people, places, and things that had an impact on one's life. My decision to write this book came from the support of all the great teachers, directors, fellow actors, family, and friends I have been fortunate enough to have known. I deeply appreciate the gift of their knowledge and support, and the encouragement they have given me throughout the years:

Anne Babson, who introduced me to the love of theatre.

WWB, who loved sweet music.

Russell Crouse, for his gift of enthusiasm.

Walker Hancock, for being my mentor for all the arts.

Jack and Al, Jill and Marty, David and Val, for the love of family.

Bob and Barbara and the Dunne clan for your good cheer.

My teachers: Shirley Surrette, Jim Young, Steve Macht, Lee Strasberg, James Burrows.

Walter Braumhoff, for kicking me out and into the real world.

Helen Chinoy, for giving me a chance at Smith and then encouraging me on.

Len Berkman, for teaching me the love of the work.

Leon Katz, for his enormous encouragement at Yale.

Kathy Kristopher, who expanded my concept of acting and teaching.

Bob Butler, my first film director, for showing me the transition.

Bob Tompson, Rod Paul and Marty Schiff, for life at the LA Film Actors Lab.

Lynn Britt, at the National Theatre Institute, a great teacher and administrator.

Michael Nash, at Emerson College, for his persistence and innovation.

Fellow actors and friends: Tots, Grant Goodeve, Faith Prince, John and Matthew Perry, John Driver, Jack Jobes, Tim Noyes, Trevor and Marcie, Ted, John, George, Rhea, Woody, and Kellsey.

My friend and great cinematographer, Emil Oster.

My editors: Laurel Moje, Leslie Kahn, Una Marcotte, Anne Babson Carter.

The Heinemann brain trust: Lisa Barnett, Vicki Kasabian, Jenny Jensen Greenleaf, and Anne Sauvé.

Dudley French Blodget, whose friendship has always made me feel like I could win.

And

Kelly Ann Dunne Babson, my partner in life's adventures—*The Actor's Choice* being a big one.

Preface

*T*his book is about *choices*. Do you have the ability, the *craft*, to choose where you practice your art? Do you want to be in a Broadway play, a fifty-million-dollar feature film, a small ninety-nine seat Equity waiver house, a sitcom, a soap, a Ty·D·Bol commercial, a cartoon, a voice-over? My intent is for you to be a working actor, to establish a real career that includes artistic fulfillment, financial security, and a normal life which allows the possibility of sending your kids to college. To accomplish that lifestyle, your stage- *and* screen-acting craft needs to be ready to take advantage of the opportunities that become available. This book tells how to refine your craft for both stage and screen so that you have the options to make those choices.

Obviously the stage has its own set of limitations that any actor faces in the preparation and performance of his art. Yet the training and experience many stage actors encounter tends to lead them to the assumption that essentially, acting is acting. What I want you to recognize in this book is that different mediums have different limitations and therefore, need different techniques. While it is true that there are certain essential elements that comprise any acting experience, it is also true that there are certain factors specific to the screen experience that are fundamentally different from those of the stage. Once those factors or inherent limitations are identified, we can work toward a way to diminish those conditions so that our work on screen can approach the depth and integrity it has on the stage.

Since the basis for any concept that functions as a system or method of acting must begin with a fundamental understanding of the medium itself, the first priority is to identify *what* the specific differences are between the stage and screen mediums. In the process we also will discover *why* these differences exist. The results should help isolate the limitations inherent to the screen experience.

This is not a beginner's book. I begin with the assumption that you are an actor, that through your training and/or experience you already have a considerable understanding of the basic concepts of acting for the theatre. I am going to challenge some of those ideas and theories, maybe even the very definition of acting. I ask you, however, for one accommodation. Please do not evaluate what you have read until the end of the book. Read with an open mind and then tear the material apart. Use what works for you and reject the rest.

My approach to screen work comes from thirty years of learning, doing, investigating, and teaching for both stage and screen, and often learning all over again. I didn't even see a camera until I'd acted and directed in over one hundred university, regional, and professional theatre productions. My bias toward stage training is evident, but it is the theatre where the vast majority of actors get their start. When I finally found my way onto the screen, I had to make the transition quickly without benefit of counsel. Today, with over two hundred film, television, and commercial credits, I have developed a way of working that speaks to the day-in and day-out struggle of the working actor—not just to the elite "movie star." With opportunities like the eleven years as the recurring character of Sam's lawyer on "Cheers," I was fortunate to have had the chance to work with some very gifted and hardworking actors. Over the years I have noticed that there is a commonality to the true actor's experience, whether the star or the day player: it is a respect for the craft and a perseverance of the art. The ideas expressed here are a culmination of all the experiences I had working with those people and the observations that came from seeing them struggle with the same acting problems you will face when you step onto a TV or film set.

What is in this book is an approach to learning how to overcome the limitations presented by the film medium by adjusting your stage-acting technique. It's not the only way successful actors work on screen—consider it a tool. We are all eclectic in our development of craft, but growth comes only if we can give up our natural insecurities about trying new ideas. Your training and experience are important and valid, but we can all achieve more beyond what we've learned and experienced if we can stay accessible.

The objectives of this book are to explore the relationship between stage and screen; to identify the limitations within the film medium; and to introduce a technique designed to confront those limiting factors. There have been vague attempts in the past to describe the film-acting experience as a separate entity from stage and to articulate their very fundamental differences. Now it's my turn!

The Technical Differences 1

*M*ost actors, especially during their first few attempts at film, will say they wish they could achieve the same quality of work on screen as they can onstage. That is the goal of this book. With the knowledge of what the technical differences are between stage and screen and, more importantly, why they exist, we can realize how these differences create limitations for the actor that can interfere with the actor's ability to achieve a well-crafted, artistically successful result on the screen.

There are two elements that an actor brings to his work: the *craft* to communicate his vision; and the *choices* he makes to communicate with that craft. How then does a screen actor create a three-dimensional performance as truthful as his brother the stage actor with little preparation or rehearsal, and little or no direction, and yet keep his performance consistent through thirty takes? There are major adjustments to be made when an actor works on screen that are dictated by the mediums' differences. These differences break down to *technical* differences and *technique* differences.

Technical differences are the limitations within either medium that are beyond the actor's control; that is, they are inherent to the medium. The best producers, directors, and actors in the world are bound by the same restrictions. Because of these technical limitations, an actor must adjust his technique.

To begin, it must be understood that the words *stage* and *screen* are, in themselves, general terms whose concept changes from genre to genre. In theatre the actor constantly adapts his technique to fit the stage he is on. Imagine performing a Mamet play in a little ninety-nine-seat Equity waiver house versus performing *Guys and Dolls* in a two thousand-seat Broadway theatre.

One of the obvious and immediate differences between stage and screen is the distance between the actor and his audience. Charles Durning talks about the difference in *Conversations in the Wings* (Heinemann, 1994), "Laurence Olivier was asked once if he had to retain only one thing for acting . . . on the screen, what would it be? And he said, his eyes. And you know, if you look at the great screen actors, they have the ability to change expression through the eyes. Look at Gary Cooper. He could make you know exactly what he was thinking." In a large theatre, the audience not only can't read what is in the actor's eyes—they often can't even see them!

Apart from the purely physical consideration of stage and theatre size, the style and period of a play dictate adjustments to accommodate the necessity of different voice and movement technique. Consider the difference in language between Shakespeare and Neil Simon. Adaptation and the ability to play different periods and styles is what regional repertory theatre is all about.

Similarly, the term *screen* is relative. There are feature films, mini-series, movies of the week (MOW), hour episodics, sitcoms, and soaps. Each of these has its own problems, its own set of limitations, and therefore its own adjustments for the actor's technique. It is, therefore, a bit simplistic to say, "the difference between stage and screen" when there is so much diversity within each medium.

Money

The major differences between theatre and film can be traced to one source: *money*. Remember, the term is show *business*. It's a business, not an art form. Almost no one involved with making films considers it an art form until Oscar or Emmy time rolls around each year. Every decision producers make, from script to casting to location, is financially based. How much will it cost? How much can we expect to get back? An actor will never actually hear the producers say, "Well, this actor would be better in the part, but so-and-so can do it and make us more money at the box office." But in fact this is how many decisions are made. The producers have careers too. And as you will see, the cost of TV and film production has a direct bearing on the actor's ability to do his job. Let's look at a comparison of the numbers.

Producing a major Broadway musical such as *Sunset Boulevard* is an expensive proposition costing about $15 million. But very few of these large-scale productions are produced each year. According to the League of American Theaters and Producers, in 1974–75 there were fifty-eight new productions as compared to the 1991–1992 season where there were twenty-seven for-profit productions, fourteen musicals, and thirteen plays. The average cost of producing a Broadway musical was $2.8 million, and $900,000 for a new play. Based on these figures, the total cost for all new commercial Broadway productions in 1992 was $52 million. $52 million! The cost of Kevin Costner's 1995 *Waterworld* was over $175 million alone!

Now look at film and television costs. According to the Motion Picture Association of America, the 1994 average feature film budget was $34 million! By the time you read this, it will probably be considerably higher. Talking with many knowledgeable industry personnel, I found that TV costs were also high. A mini-series' costs depend on the number of hours shot that go on the air. Steven King's, "The Stand" cost $28 million. A two-hour movie of the week (MOW) is close to $3 million. A one-hour episodic television show reaches $1.5 million. A half-hour sitcom can run upward of $800,000 per show. A soap opera shoots one show every day, five days a week. Because of low set costs and the use of videotape instead of film, soaps are not as expensive as episodic television and run from $125,000 for a half-hour show to $200,000 for an hour show. And, finally, the much maligned thirty-second network commercial can cost anywhere from $25,000 to $1 million.

These are staggering costs that seem only to escalate each year. The payback for the producers comes when the product hits the market and the audience pays the price of admission. Movie grosses, of course, are tracked, recorded, and analyzed in minute detail every day. Stock prices of the major studios and entertainment corporations like Disney, Time Warner, and Viacom rise and fall on the success or failure of a single film release. With television, the audience (profits) show themselves by how many people are watching a particular show in any given time slot. These numbers are the lifeblood of television and are called the Nielsen ratings.

The Nielsen company tracks how many television sets are turned on throughout the country (the rating) and how many of those sets are watching a certain show (the share). The rating and share define the popularity of a show and determine the price of the commercial time it commands. Advertising companies such as Proctor and Gamble will pay a lot more for a thirty-second spot for a top show like "Cheers," when it's rated in the top 10, than it would for a sixty-second spot for a show rated near the bottom. An episodic or a sitcom show—there are more than seventy of them—which is first in the ratings can receive more than $300,000 per minute of advertising. If there are eight minutes of advertising in the average half hour of programming and you multiply that by $300,000, you can see that networks make $2,400,000 for a show that may cost only $1,500,000 to produce. That show will then be rerun during the summer and the only costs the producers will incur are the residual payments to the writer, director, and actors.

Now let's look at the opposite situation. The lowest rated prime time shows might receive a rating of only 6 or 7 as opposed to a high rating of 32 or 33. When ratings are down, advertising dollars go down. It doesn't take long to figure out why these shows are cut after three or four episodes. The network, the producers—everybody loses money. Occasionally a network will carry a show if it thinks it can build up the audience with time, advertising, and especially good reviews. "Cheers," "M*A*S*H," and "Taxi" were each rated last in their first season. But the reviews were good and the network stuck with them.

If a show can make it through the season into the summer and reruns, the network can recoup some of its costs. And if a show manages to survive from week to week, the audience increases naturally, creating better ratings and therefore more money from advertising time. If the show can hold on long enough to qualify for syndication, the profits are larger still. A 1992 *Los Angeles Times* article titled "Too Costly for Prime Time" states, "Most prime-time network shows initially lose money for studios . . . a practice called 'deficit financing.'. . . Over a four-year period—the time it takes to produce the 88 episodes regarded as the minimum for breaking into syndication—a network sitcom can run up a deficit of $12 million. Losses on a one-hour drama can hit $30 million." But the profits can be huge—in 1988 "The Cosby Show" set the syndication record, selling for $4.4 million per episode.

Imagine the feelings of desperation that seize everyone—from producers to networks to cast and crew. Everyone questions: Will the audience materialize? Will the numbers go up? Can the show eventually pay for itself? Will I have a job next week? The point of all this is that *film and television are very expensive mediums*; money drives the medium and eventually affects the actor.

The time it takes to shoot a film or TV show also needs to be discussed because "time is money," and time, or the lack of it, creates the greatest limitation the actor faces. Feature films take two to four months to film, ninety-six-minute MOWs take seventeen to twenty-one days to shoot, and one-hour episodics take seven working days. You can begin to see the discrepancy here in the "artistic" time available to create a quality project. A sitcom takes five days to rehearse and shoot and soap operas take one day for a one-hour show.

To bring this into better perspective for the actor, let's look at how many pages of script are filmed per day. With feature films, because of the larger budgets, the script-per-day ratio is low— two pages per day. The opening scene in the movie *Reds,* which takes place in a photography gallery, was rehearsed for one week and shot over the next week. But *Reds* cost $40 million to make and took close to a year and a half to shoot.

In the case of mini-series and MOWs, approximately 10 plus pages per day are shot. Episodic shows generally manage 12 pages per day depending on the ratio of action/stunt scenes to dialogue scenes. That's a hard pace, but time is money so staying on budget depends on keeping the pages-per-day ratios high. TV directors are often judged by being on time and on budget. Half-hour soaps tape 50 pages per day; hour-long shows tape 90

	Time (minutes)	Cost	Shooting Days	Pages per Day
Feature Film	120	$34 million	2–4 months	2
MOW	96	$3 million	17–21 days	8–10
Episode	48	$1.5 million	7 days	12
Sitcom	22	$800,000	5 days	45
Soap Opera	48	$200,000	1 day	90
Commercial	.5	$100,000	1 day	1

pages. An actor with a major story line can have as many as 50 to 60 pages daily of new dialogue to memorize every day of the week, month after month. And soaps aren't rerun, they're in production all year long. The pace would kill a horse.

While working on "General Hospital" for a few days during the famous "Luke and Laura" period (1981), I asked the show's star, Tony Geary, how he was able to handle that many lines with all that pressure. He confessed that because of the incredible pace, he frequently had to improvise. During blocking and run through, from 7:30 A.M. until 10:00 or 11:30 A.M., he would go through his lines with the pages in his hands. During the dress rehearsal which was from 1:30 P.M. until 3:00 P.M. or so, he would stick the script pages under a couch or tucked away in some available hiding place in case he needed them. Then he would shoot the show from 3:30 P.M. until 7:00 P.M. or later, and whatever he retained from the rehearsal process came out.

"A couple of friends have been on soaps in big, killer parts," said Tony, "and they say the first few weeks you think you're going to die. Since most soap scenes cover the same ground over and over, it's difficult to remember what you just said the scene before the one you're working on."

These actors say you develop what the psychologists call "short-term memory." Sometimes, after they've shot a scene and the director says "Cut," they can't remember a thing. If you were to stop one of them on his way home for dinner and ask him to repeat any of the lines he spoke on camera during the day, he wouldn't remember one of them. The mind does what it has to do to survive.

Sitcoms don't relate to the pages-per-day discussion in that they rehearse for five days and shoot the night of the fifth day. They have their own set of pressures for the actor, which will be discussed later.

To equate mathematically the time it takes to shoot an average TV or film scene to the cost for a day's shooting, every take (a take is the amount of film shot between the moment the director says, "Action" and the moment he says, "Cut") is approximately one thousand dollars. Every few minutes of time cost thousands of dollars and that money/time ratio puts incredible pressure on the director, the crew, and especially the actors.

Most directors shoot five basic camera angles during the filming of each scene: a master shot, two close-ups and two over-the-shoulder shots. Then a number of takes will be shot of each angle. Remember, the director isn't only interested in the actor's work. He will be also looking at the composition of the shot, the focus, the lighting, and any camera movements. If an actor ruins an otherwise printable take—forgets a line or misses a mark—the production costs go up a thousand dollars. That's pressure! The Screen Actors Guild stipulates a minimum of $425 per day as the pay scale, and yet one mistake over the norm can cost the production one thousand dollars. That is why some producers will fly an actor all the way from Hollywood to do a small part out in the hinterlands. They want actors who know their craft and won't melt under the pressure.

The decision to use more costly actors can also be made for other reasons. For example, if the producers are casting for an actor to do a small part in a scene with Robert Redford, they don't want Redford's timing and concentration interfered with just because some neophyte is intimidated and ruins a critical take. One mistake on the part of an inexperienced actor and the cost of flying a more expensive actor out from Hollywood or New York is easily justified. Unfortunately, this constant pressure to be "Mr. One Take" can sometimes work into an inexperienced actor's subconscious and subtly coerce the individual into "playing safe," a sure path to dull and boring acting. It's happened to me and it's a horrible feeling that stays with you.

Preparation Time

With the extremely high cost of production days (days when actually shooting), the actor *must* come to the set as prepared as humanly possible. Spencer Tracy once said to a questioning young actor, "Show up on time, know your lines and don't bump into the furniture." That advice will show up over and over again because it speaks so clearly to the actor's responsibility as a professional. But that's just the craft element of preparation. There is also the preparation time that actors need to do their homework: character study, physical training, skills needed for the character—all the things stage actors take for granted during their month of rehearsal time before "opening night." Television, however, has a noticeable lack of preproduction time, namely the few days from casting until shooting begins. Most nonstarring TV roles are auditioned for on a Thursday, and cast that night, and the actors are on the set first thing Friday morning or at the latest Monday. There is no time to do any of the extended preparation work that theatre actors are accustomed to expect.

Because preparation for television and film is different from theatre, getting the most out of that day or two of preparation time becomes vital. The theatre actor is used to the luxury of time and a director who has the ability and desire to help him pull his role together. Imagine the initial shock of a trained theatre actor who shows up for the first day of rehearsal and is expected to give a final performance after one or two cursory rehearsals with a scene partner whom he's just met and whose name he's already forgotten. A stage director would never expect the actors to come in on the first day of rehearsal and be prepared to open on Broadway that night. Yet that's precisely what happens in film and television every day. That is why a different preparation technique is essential.

On the other hand, the star of an expensive feature film will probably have several months to prepare for a substantial role before the filming actually starts. Feature films are in preproduction anywhere from two to six months as compared to TV programs, which are filming twenty-four episodes a year. In television—and even in film—it pays to put a premium on what little there is of preparation time. Paul Newman, allowed the luxury of time, spent many months training for his role as a professional hockey player for the movie *Slap Shot*. For Newman, it was essential for the role that he have a fundamental understanding of the physical *and* psychological make-up of his character, Reggie, a washed-up, has-been player-coach.

Rehearsal

Because making a film is so incredibly costly, there is little time for what any theatre actor would call rehearsal. With ninety members of the cast and crew ready to shoot, and a production costing hundreds of thousands of dollars a day, it's clear that there is no time for the director to say, "OK, take five—we're going to go rehearse a little bit." That's not how they do it; they can't. A big feature film will be rehearsed only for a short period of time during preproduction. Many times the cast will get together with the director for a week before filming begins to work through the script. This is usually done around a conference table as the sets, either on location or in a sound studio, are being readied for filming and are not yet available for rehearsal. There are rare exceptions. Francis Ford Coppola took the entire cast of

Dracula away for weeks to rehearse using a variety of techniques, beginning with two full days of group reading of the original Bram Stoker novel. But for most directors there is no time for this luxury of preproduction rehearsal. It's arrive on the set, set up the scene, shoot it, on to the next. Boom! Boom! Boom!

Every once in a while fellow actors may be willing to work on a scene. But this is catch as catch can and depends on the medium, the time the actors can grab, and the willingness of the individual actors involved. Even actors who themselves come from the stage and who are used to the rehearsal process come to realize that rehearsal in the film medium is a significantly different and incomplete experience. Sir Anthony Hopkins said of the film rehearsal period, "I never like to rehearse too much because it's never the same when you get on the set." The actor's visual dependence on locations, action, and possible special effects tends to limit the rehearsal experience to the point that some actor's definition of rehearsing is running lines for memorization purposes. The idea of working and discussing a scene never enters their minds.

Some directors, after blocking a scene and while the lighting and camera preparations are being done, will take the actors aside and say, "OK, guys, let's go off to the side and let's work on this scene a little." Once you've been on the set and seen the action, rehearsal would really be valuable. But during my experience of over one hundred television shows only four directors took advantage of that opportunity. The old enemy time once again reared its ugly head. In other film genres, special effects can render rehearsal completely useless. How can an actor and director sitting around a table rehearse many of the scenes from *E.T.* or *Jurassic Park*? In *Hook* Julia Roberts played Tinkerbell in front of a blue screen on a sound stage and then was inserted in many of her scenes in postproduction. With so much physical action and special effects having nothing to do with reality, she rarely saw her fellow actors. The bottom line is don't expect rehearsal time. If you get any at all, count yourself lucky.

For most of us actors, the concept of rehearsal normally includes a process of scene preparation between the actor and director. This usually involves an exploration of the elements that are fundamental to most theatre actors' preparation and rehearsal process. The unsuspecting stage actor arriving in Hollywood—a professional with significant stage experience, completely prepared to work—is shocked to find himself woefully out of his element when he finally lands a screen role and shows up on a soundstage.

With no preparation and little rehearsal the actor thinks, "God, if we could only rehearse this scene, just a couple of times. If we could just work on it a little bit, it would be so much better." And the producer's answer? "We haven't got the time [translation: money]. We'll take care of it in post [production]. We'll fix it in editing."

The sitcom is the closest in form to the process of theatre. But while sitcoms are rehearsed for a week and actually shot in chronological order like a play in front of a live audience, rest assured that they have their own inherent obstacles. Cast in a sitcom, an inexperienced actor might say, "I'm home. I can rehearse, the pressure's off. I've got a whole week to make this work." Incorrect assessment! Wrong conclusion! Lack of time affects the actor in a more subtle way in sitcoms. When the writers (of "Cheers," for example,) first hear the script read-through with actors on a Wednesday morning, they, as well as the director, want to know if the writing works. An actor may think, "I can make this work. I've got a few days, I'll make it work." But in reality the writers want to see it work right then and there because after the actors leave the reading, the writers go back to work and more times than not, rewrite the entire script based on what worked or did not work during that first reading.

On Thursday, the actors get the new script printed on a different colored paper with any changes from the past script indicated by an asterisk marked in the margins. "Oh no!" cries the actor, "my lines have been cut—that great bit, it's gone. All my good jokes—gone!" Why? The producers and writers didn't think the lines were funny because the actor didn't make them work the first time. So now those lines are gone. Every day, actors come in and quickly examine the new pages to see how many of their lines are still in there. The director blocks what remains in the script and works through for the rest of the day. But sometimes—it's happened to most actors at least once—the dreaded phone call comes from the actor's agent, "They don't need you anymore. They've cut your character out all together." Or worse, "They recast the role." This rehearse-run through-rewrite process will continue through the week, all the way up to dress rehearsal, and perhaps even past that.

On the afternoon of shooting day, an actor can expect to do a dress rehearsal, eat dinner, then return for makeup and hair. During this time the writers fine-tune the show down to the final minute. After dinner, it is not unusual for actors to be given new material—words they've never seen before—to say in front of a live audience while filming. Sometimes the script goes back to the original lines or lines from past rewrites. Frequently, the producers and director will let the audience decide. If the audience laughs, they will leave the lines in. If it doesn't, they may rewrite, rehearse, then reshoot that portion of the show after the audience is gone. They don't like to do this, however, because they prefer the immediacy of the audience response (there are mikes all through the audience—no laugh track on most shows). So with sitcoms, yes, there is rehearsal, but with a decided edge.

What it comes down to is that the stage actor has to develop a methodology to work within the time frame of a medium that doesn't allow for much, if any, rehearsal time.

Directors

For most actors, the relationship to the director is one of the most fundamental and significant elements in the creation and development of a successful and artistically truthful performance. Most theatre actors are used to directors who are somewhat intelligent, are somewhat well read, know a little bit about the history of theatre and its literature, and might even know who Sartre is. Directors in film and television, on the other hand, come from a variety of backgrounds. They're former screen writers, story editors, editors, friends of the producer, people with money, assistant directors, production assistants, and so on. The term *director*, in the normal theatre sense, is a euphemism. It doesn't necessarily mean someone who knows how to work with actors or has any idea what a transition, subtext, or motivation is. It's rare to find a film or television director who comes from a theatre background. Directors tend to be people who know camera angles, focal lengths, composition, editing, lighting, and other mass amounts of technical minutia. Someone who can get the job done on time and under budget. Just remember the often-told joke: the actor asks the director, "What's my motivation?" and the director replies, "Your job!"

Obviously there are highly talented, artistic directors in all aspects of film and television. James Burrows of "Cheers," "Fraiser," and "Friends" comes from a theatre family: his father, Abe Burrows, was one of Broadway's greatest producers. With that experience and background in the traditions of the theatre, Burrows has been successful in every medium he's worked. His sense of pacing and timing is flawless, and he always gives his actors just the right adjustment when they need it. In the eleven years I watched him direct on "Cheers," I never saw him lose his quiet, focused control over everything that was happening on the set—even when all hell was breaking loose. But for every Burrows, there are many directors who can not give their actors the guidance and support they might need.

Oliver Stone, director of *Platoon*, *Born on Fourth of July*, and *Heaven & Earth*, works closely with his actors, although he clearly understands the symbiotic nature of the camera and the artist when he says, "Film is determined by where you put the camera . . . the camera is intricate to the film process . . . it's myself, the camera and the actor."

Hitchcock was notorious for his treatment of actors. There are many stories about what he thought about the great "art" of acting. He was known to have said, "Ninety-nine percent of my work is done at my desk." Hitchcock knew every image that he wanted on the screen, blocked out every shot on storyboards before filming began, and then would cast actors whose public personas were exactly what he wanted. He didn't have to direct Cary Grant. He hired the actor because Cary Grant was going to put Cary Grant on the screen. Hitchcock knew exactly what Cary Grant was going to do, so he would map out just what Cary Grant would look like in every one of those scenes and shoot them. He had the reputation of treating actors like cattle but knew that images told the story and he was a master storyteller. There were seventy-six edited shots in the famous shower scene from *Psycho*. Every one came from a storyboard Hitchcock created before he ever saw an actor on a soundstage.

There is also the director who never even talks to actors. I have worked on TV shows where the director never said one word to me for a whole week other than to block out a scene and say, "Action!" or "Cut!" And there are directors who are wonderful: patient and communicative, what are called "actor's directors." In the short period of time that they have to set up and shoot, they work extremely hard to get an artistically truthful scene—even in a schlocky, episodic piece of drivel.

As a screen actor, however, you must be able to work under the worst conditions and rely on your own instincts; you must be self-directed, by doing what Lee Strasberg called "developing your own critical eye." When something's not working, you have to be able to figure out why and fix it. Be aware, get on that set, and carefully watch how the director works with other actors. Once it is understood how the director wants to work with you, then you may feel comfortable asking any questions that come to mind. If he is a normal television director, however, harassed by the lack of time and under enormous pressure, it is best not to ask what your motivation or subtextual transition might be—the director's answer might be rather startling.

Scripts

The fundamental concept of the script, its structure and what it conveys to the actor, presents yet another significant contrast between stage and screen. Both mediums have storytelling in common. The technique for storytelling in each medium, however, is vastly different. Film, and by extension television, are visual. Think about that for a moment. Think about the experience of viewing a play versus a movie. A play is roughly 80 percent verbal. Eighty percent of the information the audience receives is through the words they hear coming from the actors on stage. The physical action contributes only 20 percent. In movies, however, the audience is told the story through images cut together to form a visual experience. There is sound, but the primary force of the medium is the images. These statistics are not empirical and can change from genre to genre. The television screen is relatively small compared to the movie screen and therefore less visual, so television tends to be slightly more verbal. This is especially true of soaps where there is little use of location or action and more emphasis on "talking heads." But the visual-verbal relationship consitutes a major difference between stage and screen, and the implications to the actor are important.

Think of Shakespeare's *Macbeth*. Agreed, there are various fight scenes and the occasional murder "most foul," but for the audience, it is the language, the poetry, the most skillful use of the written word in recorded history that creates the lasting allure. Through periods and styles, Shakespeare, Ibsen, Brecht, Sartre, Williams, Shepard are all playwrights, all wordsmiths. The operative word, however, is *word*. A play can be read as a piece of literature. For Sam Shepard, who has written and acted for both stage and screen, theatre will always be a refuge. In a 1994 *New York Times* article on the opening of his new play, *Simpatico* he spoke about writing for the stage: "For one thing, [theatre] allows you to explore language, which film doesn't. Film is anti-language."

A blind person can hear a play on tape and be transported by the words alone. For the stage actor, vocal techniques such as articulation, enunciation, breath control, and projection are fundamental to the craft. Get the magnificent words out to the audience. True, the words still have to be motivated. They have to be truthful. But most of all, they must be heard to be understood because with the physical limits of the stage, it is words that create the life on that stage.

In contrast, a screenplay by its very form tends not to be literature. Though screenwriters go into a frenzy when I say this, the reality is that most scripts written for television and film would in no way be properly described as literature. This is a controversial subject as screenwriters have traditionally come up short in the writer/director/actor power struggle because of the "art by committee" approach to filmmaking. In theatre, the playwright's words are protected by union contract, whereas in film and television they are not. The screenwriter submits his script and by the time it's rewritten by any number of writers, producers, or directors, and then shot and edited, the final form can sometmes bear little or no resemblance to the original script. It can be a frustrating and demeaning process that strips the writer of any control over his own art.

This is not to imply that screenplays are not an art form or that they are void of literary value. The success of any film or television project depends heavily on the script and good writing. Ask anyone on "Cheers" and they will tell you that the reason the show was as good as it was, for as long as it was, was due to the skill of the writers. The *New York Times* magazine published an article in 1995 entitled, "The Triumph of the Prime Time Novel" by Charles McGrath, which stated "TV will never be better than reading, thank goodness. And images and spoken words, no matter how eloquent, lack the suggestiveness the invitation to something deeper, of words on a page. But on television these days, if you listen hard enough, you can often hear dialogue of writerly quality—dialogue, that is, that's good enough to be in a book. . . . A few of the more inventive series, for example, have become for our era the equivalent of the serial novel."

A screenplay, more than a stage play, needs to be translated from a written medium to a visual medium for the average person to understand and appreciate. An analogy would be for that same person to look at a written score of a Bach concerto. If she can't read music, it's not music. If you get bogged down in the morass of physical description of setting and action that permeates a screenplay, you will have difficulty reading it with any sense of a through line. In some instances, it's almost unintelligible. When it is readable, it is often missing much of the subtext or is just plain mediocre writing. One isn't inclined to nestle in front of a warm fire to enjoy a screenplay.

It's important to understand that this general discussion comes from the actor's point of view and relates to the *entire* spectrum of screenplays written for film *and* television; not just for the few great films that come out every once in a while. Look at the numbers. In 1994 there were fewer than four hundred films produced and released. Of those I would guess you might find ten or twenty that would qualify for the term literature. Past films like *Howard's End, Raging Bull, The Pawnbroker, The Madness of King George, Some Like It Hot, The Big Sleep, Bicycle Thief, Blow Up, Singin' in the Rain, Manhattan,* or *Schindler's List* would be very interesting to read. Remember that there is more chance of a film script being well written than a television script because statistically there is more time in preproduction to write and rewrite.

The frenetic pace of television produces sixty to seventy series every week, each averaging twenty-two episodes a year for twelve hundred scripts. Ten soap operas contribute five shows a week, fifty weeks a year adding another 2,500 more. Conservatively, that's more than 3,700 individual television scripts a year. For every award-winning Hallmark Hall of Fame presentation, special movie of the week, or great episode of "NYPD Blue," "Cheers," "ER," or "M*A*S*H," how many would anyone classify as literature? I can tell you that in twenty years of working as an actor in more than two hundred films and television shows, very, very few of those scripts would be considered literature. Good writing? Sometimes, yes. Even great writing once in a while. But literature? I really don't think you can equate a "Beverly Hills 90210" script with *Romeo and Juliet* or *West Side Story.* It's not a fair comparison. Literature is meant to be read, while screenplays are meant to be experienced visually.

A screenplay is a *verbal* representation of a *visual* medium; the screenwriter has to describe to the reader the images that tell the story. Good screenwriters use *visual language* to create stories in the readers' minds. The actor's job is to translate this visual language into the character's behavior that can then be captured as images on film.

When directors read a script, they too are translating the printed page into images. They see shot sequences that cut into other shots that ultimately become a scene. Hitchcock started from page one of the script, as he once described, "writing down images, no matter how tiny, that became, like the tiny dots of music, a symphony of wonderful music." Not a word was spoken in the famous *Psycho* shower scene. The audience was reduced to shock and screams by a manipulation of images that created a much gorier scene in their minds than was actually shot. As a matter of fact, at no time did the knife actually make contact with Janet Leigh. So the screen actor has to understand that his work is oftentimes not verbal. His work is subtextual and emotional, what is thought and what is felt, because that is what the audience reads through the images.

Brian Dennehy was correct when he said, "On stage I per- form, on the screen I behave." That's the difference in the prover- bial nutshell. For the actor, it is *behavior* that visually translates the language with which the director is telling his story. By behav- ior I mean what a character *does* as well as says; words *and* actions. This is demonstrated in Holly Hunter's Academy Award- winning portrayal of a mute in *The Piano*. Without words her actions say all that is needed. Or with a verbal but reserved char- acter like Lawrence in *Lawrence of Arabia*, we understand him through his behavior, not just his words. The scene of O'Toole's interrogation by Jose Ferrer as the Turkish officer was a brilliant use of the subtextual and emotional levels that dictate behavior.

In a love scene on stage the actors will talk about what they think and feel about themselves or each other. But on screen, the couple may wash the dishes and the actress may say, "Pass me the towel . . . here's a dish you didn't get clean enough." And it's a love scene. The emotion comes through the behavior, not the words.

The length of a scene is yet another difference between a stage play and a screenplay. While it would not be uncommon to find a fifteen- to twenty-page scene in a play, a long TV or film scene is barely over two or three pages in length. Scenes are sometimes one or two images—no words, just images.

Film projects based on materials from other mediums some- times find their way to the screen. This process is known as an *adaptation.* Novels, short stories, and plays have been adapted to film and television since the beginning of the medium. In looking at what is involved in translating a stage play into a screenplay, there's usually a discussion about "opening up" the play to make it more visual, in order to create more physical action in one form or another. What producers are concerned with is the play's inherently verbal presentation and lack of visual input. Adaptations of successful plays must find a way to translate the essence of the play into a visual representation.

The industry's prevalent philosophy considers stageplay adaptations risky and usually unsuccessful because of their poor track record. Yet most adaptations have done badly at the box office because the producers and writers are so impressed with the play that they forget they are working in a totally different format and that the play needs to be rewritten for a visual medium. And writers continually complain, "You don't mean you're going to *change* that brilliant work of art? Why it's a Pulitzer Prize (or Tony Award) winner!"

The adaptation of *Children of a Lesser God* is a case in point. Mark Medoff had written the first screenplay from his original award-winning play. When Randa Haines was hired to direct, she made it clear there were inherent problems in the play that had to be dealt with in order to get it on the screen. For one thing, only the lead male character had most of the lines, and he said not only his lines but, while translating the other major character's sign language, hers as well. Haines also had to accommodate the fact that everyone was using sign language by pulling the camera back in order to see all the hand movements. She knew she had to forget about the original play's structure and create a new point of view that worked for the screen. She did just that, but not before having to let Medoff go and hire another writer who would go along with her concept. She was vilified by the writing community for her action. She was proven right, however, when the film came out, received tremendous reviews, and Marlee Matlin won an Academy Award. Actually, many feel the material worked better as a film than as a Broadway play.

Amadeus is another good example of understanding the medium and allowing the producers, writers, and directors a free hand at creating a piece that works in the film medium. But more often than not, the work just doesn't lend itself to the screen. *Equus* the play was a brilliantly conceived piece of theatre—emotionally powerful, psychologically disturbing, and full of both intensely riveting dialogue and wonderfully visual conventions. Richard Burton performed both the stage and the film productions, but there was absolutely no comparison. *Equus* the film was heavy, plodding, and uninspired. It lost all its immediacy and electricity. Same dialogue, same actor—different medium.

For you the actor, the most important thing to understand about a film script is that in your preparation and work it is not a literary masterpiece that should be worshipped like an icon. It is a tool of your craft, a guidepost to developing the character's behavior. Screenwriting is an art form as are acting and directing. It is the collaborative nature of film and television that creates the final product that results on the screen.

Typecasting

The industrywide use of typecasting—although frustrating for the actor—exists for two simple and very good reasons: the first is *time*. There isn't enough time in a twenty-two-minute (eight minutes for commercials) TV show to tell the audience why the intern is a one-eyed, lisping, Jewish Puerto Rican. It might make for interesting casting, but the folks in Indiana won't have a clue as to what is going on. The point is that in visual language, exposition kills. Characters standing around "explaining" themselves or the situation creates boredom. So the actor playing an intern must instantly be recognizable as what the average person expects an intern to look like or there is an interruption of rhythm and continuity. The other reason for typecasting is the camera. The camera is so close that, unless it is essential to the story that the star age or play some physically different character, makeup is not an option on screen. It is done all the time on stage because the stage has an aura of illusion, and an actor is limited only by his talent. Not so, unfortunately, on screen. Parts are lost because the actor is an inch too tall, an inch too short, too light, dark, "New England," old, young, athletic, good looking, homely, and so on. (I was once told I wasn't right for the part because my chin was too square.) At times it can be extremely frustrating. But the point is, when a Bo Derek is needed for the movie *10*, Meryl Streep with all her talent and ability isn't going to be able to create the physical presence needed for that part.

The good news is an actor will be able to draw on a great deal of physical reality from fellow actors in a scene. The older lady who plays a grandmother will look like a real grandmother. She won't be a thirty-five-year-old actress with makeup plastered on her face. And if the part calls for great beauty, it can be seen, touched, and felt. The Beauty might not be able to act as well as her stage counterpart, but she will be physically perfect for the part.

Crews and Equipment

Crews and equipment can be a major source of distraction, confusion, and interference for the film actor's concentration. Onstage, the crew is hidden and silent (the equipment is part of the set or hidden in the wings) and the actors are comfortable with their environment. By performance time, the actors are rehearsed, they've known their lines and blocking for many weeks, and they've worked out all the technicalities. When opening night comes, there is only the actor and the audience. The show stays basically the same: the size and the quality of the audiences vary. Barring disaster, the set and everything that is done each night remain constant.

When an actor works on a soundstage, things change constantly. Except for television series that use the same sets from week to week, every day is foreign. The whole theatrical concept of really knowing your set is nonexistent—there isn't time. A screen actor may be shooting a scene within minutes of seeing the set for the first time. There are ninety technicians, equipment, lights, cables, microphones, and other distractions everywhere.

An actor, standing on his mark ready for an important close-up in a love scene, may face something like the following scenario: the makeup person is busy dusting off his face, and wardrobe is straightening out the clothes while the cinematographer is saying, "OK, now raise your head a little, up a little, tilt your head that way, now, I'm going to put an inky [a small light] in your eye so that your eye sparkles." The actor must hold this uncomfortable physical position until the lights are adjusted and the cinematographer says, "Now—I'm ready." Then the director says, "Action!" Not a great deal of romantic ambiance!

Or consider this scenario: the other actor in the scene, for some reason or another, isn't available for the actor's close-up. The script supervisor reads the actor's line (in monotone)—"I love you, darling, you are my life"—and the cameraman holds his hand out to the side of the lens and says, "Do your lines to my hand. Right there. The light's perfect." The director calls, "Action!" The actor must respond.

Depending on health, age, and availability of cast members, you sometimes have to work while a critical member is missing. Fred McMurray in the old TV series, "My Three Sons" worked so many days a week and so many weeks a season, so the producers did whole shows where all his masters and close-ups were shot. The crew came back to shoot all the close-ups of the other actors in the scenes days, weeks, or sometimes months later. The other actors wouldn't even know what episode they were on. "Oh, remember that show that we did about Ernie and the dog? Yeah, well, we're going to do your close-up from that." Then the editor would put all the pieces together in post-production.

During the first season on "Paper Chase," actor John Houseman was getting along in years. His memory and stamina diminishing, he could only work six hours a day for three days a week. Consequently, all of his shots were done first. If time ran out and he had to leave, the other actors would have to do their close-ups without him.

In film and television, concentration is essential because the actor is constantly starting and then being stopped. And because each scene is shot many times from different angles, the actor must have the control to release his character's emotions from one take so that he can begin again with a clean slate on the next take. In the theatre, it's curtain up, light the lights, do the show from beginning to end, curtain down, thank you, and good night. Film isn't done that way. It's almost always shot completely out of chronological order. Henry Fonda said about performing for the theatre, "I loved saying the words from beginning to end." In film, the actor shows up on the set the first day and might be doing the last scene of the script.

For time and money's sake, a film's exterior locations are usually shot first, interiors last (if it rains, the production can move inside and the exterior shots rescheduled). All the bedroom scenes are shot at one time, then all the living room scenes, and so on. These scenes could appear at different ends of the script—and, in the story's chronological time, maybe months or years apart. The actor must be able to make the jump in time so that the character's transition is believed. More and more directors, especially of feature films, would love to have the time and money to shoot in chronological order—so would the actors, for that matter.

Pressure

Because time is money and both are at a premium, there is a tremendous amount of pressure for everyone—especially the actor. At the very moment when actors should relax, take their time, and think of nothing but their work, the pressure to "get it done fast" can destroy concentration, create nervous tension, and severely limit an actor's performance.

In filming an episode of "240 Robert" (a late 70s ABC search-and-rescue series), the cast and crew were down on the piers at San Pedro, California, filming on a big cargo ship. The light was fading and there were two more shots left to do using the ship as the background. The problem was that the ship was leaving for Japan that night so those shots *had* to get done fast, as there was no tomorrow. The pressure not to make a mistake was intense. That's when professionals who know their craft are needed. Directors get rehired if they come in under time and under budget. With that thought in mind and his back to the wall, the director drove the crew: "Everything is fine, let's just do it! OK, Action!" "This is wrong, that's wrong," people protested. "No, forget it," the director yelled. "Shoot the damn scene!" At those times, the actor just prays, "Dear God, let me show up on time, know my lines and not bump into the furniture." Opening night on Broadway has its share of pressure because a bad performance can mean the closing of the play. But the pressure during filming, especially under such time constraints, is intense and unrelenting.

Other Actors

Working relationships with other actors are a fragile thing in any medium. It helps considerably if one is thrown into a situation with good people. Waiting in the honey wagon (dressing rooms in trailers) on the show "Lou Grant," I was just getting organized when Ed Asner knocked on the door and said, "I saw you come in. I'm Ed and I wanted to introduce myself. We're in a scene together and I want you to know that my cubicle is right next to yours. Anytime you want to rehearse, the door's open. Any questions you have, ask." That was the attitude that permeated the set. "Let's work together and get this done right." (Not all sets are like that. Wonder Woman never came knocking on my door.) Ed treated everyone the same. "If you have time, let me introduce you to the other guys in the scene with us," he said. We met and talked about the scene and read it over once. "If you guys are happy with this," he said, "Let's wait until the director blocks the scene to see what else we're going to do."

When a scene is blocked, it can change. Lines may be added or cut, physical business created, even character motivations altered. No one is ever quite sure what's going to happen with a script until the actor is on the set and actually shooting the scene. Even though the actor may have an idea of how a scene will play, the reality can be considerably different.

After our scene was blocked Ed came over and said, "Gee, Tom, I see the way he's blocking it now and you've got a speech here, where the editor is going to want to cut away in the middle of that to get a reaction shot and he's not going to have the room [time] to get back to you. If I were you, I'd motivate some kind of pause in there so that the editor can cut back to you. The scene is yours and the focus [the camera] really should be on you." I was just worrying about getting the lines and blocking down. "Pausing for edit cuts?" I thought. "You've got to be kidding." But Ed was right. It was shot that way, and that's exactly how the editor cut it. That's how well Ed knows his craft. And that's why Ed's shows have had more quality than many others of that genre.

The problem for the actors is that there is little or no time to develop a relationship with one another. As a series regular on television or in a major film role, there is time to get to know the people you work with. But a day or week player shows up, performs, and leaves. Many times he'll never even have a conversation with the other actors in the scene. The process for sitcoms like "Cheers" *is* different. Because rehearsal is five days and filming is on the last day, there tends to be time when the cast sits around waiting to rehearse. The pressure of filming isn't felt until the last day, so the cast and crew are relaxed and friendly. Some "stars" don't mix with the guest cast, but on "Cheers," Ted Danson made sure everyone was included, whether you wanted to be or not (especially when it came to his practical jokes). He and the other regulars wanted a relaxed set so that the guest actors would do their best work and not play safe. They knew actors can't work well if they're scared to make a mistake or if they're intimidated by the other actors in the scene. On stage, the actor has the whole rehearsal period to deal with those insecurities. On a set, he may have just moments.

Camera

The most misunderstood difference between stage and screen and the reason why the mediums are so technically different is the camera. The camera is so invasive it can read thoughts and emotions. On a large 70-millimeter feature-film screen, each of the actor's eyes could be five feet wide. Jody Foster said of Richard Donner, director of *Maverick*, "When he's looking at me through the camera, it feels like he's inside my face, not just looking at my face." And the audience sees what the camera can see: into the actor's soul. Everything reads; a little thought crosses the mind says volumes. Compared to what that camera reads, the stage is like looking at people from the top of a ten-story building. For many actors, the theatre experience is more artistically rewarding on many levels, but in terms of the variety of choices available to the actor—the nuances, the layering of emotions, and the subtlety of characterization—the screen offers much more potential.

The visual image on screen is everything. When the cameraman wants something from the actor—a head tilted a certain way, the body placed in certain position, a certain pace of walking, he gets what he wants. One of the liberating aspects of the film medium is that many times an actor has the physical freedom of movement (in the larger scope of location) which allows him to be completely real and natural. Unlike the stage actor who is restricted by the physical limitations of the stage itself (try doing *Lawrence of Arabia* or *Indiana Jones* on stage), the screen actor usually need worry only about behaving like his character would. But there are times when the actor will have to curb what feels natural in order to accommodate the technical limitations of the camera and its lenses.

I once shot a scene in which I walked in front of a row of buildings. The camera followed my action, rolling beside me on a track. My character was supposed to be frustrated and upset as he walked with a fast, aggressive gait. The cameraman said to the director, "We're striating with this lens, so have the actor go about one-third slower." That can be a little disconcerting to a theatre actor. The whole point of stage acting is to be spontaneous, to play the now and be fresh in the immediacy of it. If the actor crosses or makes a turn differently every night, who cares? As long as he hits his light and doesn't alter the basic blocking of the director, moment-to-moment acting is rewarded.

Screen actors, however, have a technical limitation that is unique to the medium: *matching takes*. Whatever behavior (movement, subtext, or emotion) was done in the master shot must be matched in the close-up, over-the-shoulder, two-shot, etc. The editor's nightmare is an actor who can't match takes. If an editor can't cut between a two-shot and an over-the-shoulder shot because the actor isn't doing the same things (the images won't align), then he is limited in his ability to do his job successfully and creatively. Notice that there are Oscars for editing too!

Physical Reality

Now and again, the physical components of a film set are of such a degree of realness that they become a source of motivation for the actor. This concept, unique to the screen, is called *physical reality*, and comprises three elements: the script, the other actors, and the environment (setting). On "Cheers," actors said lines that were completely natural (real), drank real beer (nonalcoholic), ate real pretzels, and sat at a real working bar talking to other actors who looked exactly like their characters. The point is, except for the audience and the technical crew out there, the actors felt as though they were in a real bar. Whereas, if it were a stage production, the set would be opened and tilted such that the audience could see it better. From the audience's view it would look real, but from the actor's point of view, it would be grossly overpainted and give the actor no assistance in creating a sense of reality.

Consider, for example, a production of Shakespeare in the round, where the actor must perform on a unit set with elementary platforms and risers instead of scenery. His lines are metered Elizabethan poetry. The actor playing Othello opposite him is nowhere near the right age or nationality and is "painted up" to look the part. The total sum of the physical reality available to help this actor is zero. (The other side of this equation, however, is that the theatre actor playing Othello is probably a terrific actor, making up for whatever is lacking in physical reality by his wonderful performance.)

On a soundstage, or better yet on location, actors can draw on any number of sensory elements that are of enormous help in achieving "realness." The script's dialogue is beyond realism; it's ultra-naturalistic. The actors are perfectly typecast so a grandmother will look like the perfect grandmother, a tough killer, will look mean and intimidating, and a beautiful woman will be a beautiful woman.

Because of its naturalism and because the costs of renting soundstages and building complex sets are so high, more and more filming is done on location in real places. When a hospital set is needed, the producers go to a real hospital. On the ABC series "240-Robert," the cast and crew never went to a sound-stage in a whole year of shooting. The truth is, using real locations helps the actor tremendously. Walking into real woods, touching real trees, and hearing the sounds of nature allow the actor to build from the physical reality surrounding him. The five senses become a powerful tool. As a result, half the work is done—*if* the actor can take advantage of it.

Filmwork, however, can have a degree of stylization that wreaks havoc on physical reality. Imagine the technical difficulty for Bob Hoskins in *Who Framed Roger Rabbit?* Almost all his scenes were done with nonexistent characters who appeared in the film as animation. (Once playing a bad guy on "Wonder Woman" I had to say the immortal line, "Take that, Wonder Woman!" So much for script physical reality.)

Accepting Limitations

The final point on the technical difference between stage and screen is *once it's shot, it's forever!* I did a low-budget feature film called *Beasts*. That film will haunt me for generations to come. Whereas, if you've ever been in a stinker play, the two good things about it are it's over once it's over, and very few people ever saw or will remember it.

Whether you find yourself in a low-budget film like *Beasts* or an Academy Award-winning film like *Schindler's List*, you are in a position to realize the ample rewards of the film industry. And if you do so, don't whine or complain about how terrible the script was, how long the day was, how bad the director was, or how there was no time for your "art." If you can't stand the limitations, stay out of the biz! For me, *Beasts* is still out there. You be the judge.

The Technique Differences 2

Over the years, many actors of vastly different backgrounds have tried to articulate what it is they do—and have failed in the attempt. For some, their acting technique has taken such a circuitous route in its development that to surgically open it up to the light of reason is difficult at best, possibly even harmful. Every once in a while, however, an actor will answer a question about the acting process with a casual remark that turns out to be a revelation that defines the very nature of his art. In a *Life* magazine article on the movies a number of years back, Brian Dennehy made just such a simple and incontrovertible comment when he said, "On stage I perform, on camera I behave." This is an illusive distinction that has its origins in the nature of the stage and screen mediums.

The next step is to look at the basic constructs of the actor's technique, or craft, to better understand the adjustments necessary to overcome, or at least lessen, the limitations imposed by the film medium. Remember, the limitations are inherent to the medium. To some extent they exist no matter what the quality of the project or the talent and skill of the people directing and producing that project are.

Emotional

Any discussion of technique differences begins with the emotions because emotional truth is the foundation of any performance. That is as true on screen as it is onstage. A method actor at heart, I believe in working from the inside out. I studied with Lee Strasberg and, although some of my ideas disagree with his, his basic tenet of emotional truth has always shown itself to be an accurate guideline whether an actor is doing Ibsen, "Cheers," "General Hospital," "Wonder Woman," *Forest Gump* or a Budweiser commercial. The medium and genre may change, but the foundation must always be emotional reality.

The Method and Strasberg have had their share of detractors over the years. Many industry people have a very stilted view of its tenets and practices. Don Richardson, an apprentice to the Group Theatre, advises against the Method in his book, *Acting Without Agony,* when he says, "I believe acting is a work of the imagination. . . . Art is a reflection of reality itself, not reality itself. . . the Method doesn't work. It is an outdated concept that isn't practical for the way an actor must work today. . . . It insists on delving into the actor's personal life in ways that I consider unprofessional. . . . It results in tedious, neurasthenic performances. . . . This results in endless cruelty and quackery that go on in lofts and drama schools like the Strasberg Institute." He then goes on to ridicule actors like Dustin Hoffman, Nicholas Cage, Marlon Brando, and Nick Nolte for their use of Method type preparation in their work.

What Mr. Richardson and others prefer to misunderstand is that the only thing the Method is trying to accomplish is emotional truth. It uses innumerable pathways to get to that truth including simple basic believability through the actor's imagination. It also has many different sense memory exercises that can be of benefit when an actor needs them. It by no means calls for the actor to, as Richardson states, "shoot yourself up to play a drug addict."

My place is not to be a Method apologist here. As I said from the beginning, we are all eclectic in our process and most actors I know and have read about, onstage or screen, will go anywhere (technique) to get to where they want to go (truth).

So what is the difference? It's that invasive little lens again. Mother Nature can't be fooled and neither can the camera. Look at the difference between the emotional range, depth and believability of Robert De Niro in *Raging Bull* and Lee Majors in—anything.

Obviously there's a huge contrast in ability, but there also is a huge difference in the mediums and genres they work in. We have come to accept less from television and its actors then we do from film. We also accept less from certain genres of film than others. Does Arnold Schwarzenegger have any idea what emotional layering is when he's playing one of his action roles? Many of the lesser actors working today get by on *attitudes* rather than true emotions. The martial arts action star, Jean-Claude Van Damme once defined his acting technique as, "visual acting . . . expression of the face." Watching his work on film, he obviously means an external approach. Admittedly, viewers go to action movies for excitement and entertainment, not for the star's acting prowess. But unless an actor sees himself as the next Rambo, the goal for most actors is real emotions and emotional truth.

The technical aspects of film, with camera close-ups and the microphone inches away, provide a film actor with the wonderful opportunity to work for the most subtle nuances of emotional levels. With the camera that close, everything reads. Acting choices can be made for the camera that a stage audience in even the smallest theatres would never see. That's the difference—more *choice*.

But with that wonderful freedom of choice comes a comparable set of restrictions. Remember the restriction of time (preparation and rehearsal)? Well, the lack of time plays havoc for the actor working with the ephemeral nature of emotions. He has to develop the ability to make emotional adjustments very quickly and then repeat them take after take after take. One of the easiest ways to spot a theatre actor new to the screen is that two hours after a wonderful spontaneous performance in a master, having filmed each camera angle dozens of times, he can't match his takes on his close-ups. Often he ends up doing something very different, like trying to be spontaneous on every take or imitating what he did the two hours before on his master shot. All the life and emotional truth can vanish quickly under such circumstances. That's why editors go crazy. The craftless actor can't match his takes (emotionally this time), so the choices available to the editor are severely limited.

In referring to *matching* as regards the actor, I'm talking about matching not only the *emotional tone*, that is, layered emotions, but also matching the *intensity* of those layered emotions. When there are a number of emotions going on at the same time, some will be felt more intensely than others. Certain emotions will spark or flare up, then recede, while others intensify. Craft plays an important role here because the screen actor has to be able to repeat sequential emotions, not just imitate them but actually feel them and their intensity over and over again, in take after take. Michael Caine, in his book *Acting in Film*, points out, "In addition to being aware of visual continuity, the truly professional film actor has to be aware of emotional continuity. In the theatre, a play flows along in sequence, allowing each actor to feel the emotional build. . . . In the cinema the end result may be more realistic, but the process is definitely more artificial."

An emotional transition is one of the most powerful moments captured on film. It can be extremely subtle and brief or it can be a profound moment that dominates a scene. The actor who has control and consistency has the edge. Look at some of the stronger emotional scenes from *Raging Bull* or Jack Nicholson's courtroom speech from *A Few Good Men* or Daniel Day-Lewis' work in *In the Name of the Father* or Meryl Streep in *The Bridges of Madison County*. The one common denominator is that they all have moments that are emotionally based. Emotional moments take a great deal of craft and the problem for the actor almost always stems from the lack of time to prepare. Actors new to film will often say they could have done more, done it better, or gone deeper—if there'd been more time.

Movement

On screen, everything reads. If a physical gesture or a movement is larger than what is real (natural), or if it is projected or pushed in any way, it will read artificially. The stage actor must learn to be comfortable doing nothing, a frustrating exercise for actors who have spent years developing a craft that will allow them to use movement as a valuable tool to "take stage" or create focus whenever they wish. On screen the camera creates the focus. The actor does nothing except behave and live the life of the character at all times.

Another challenge for the theatre actor is *blocking*. Actors on stage have many weeks to work out their blocking and stage business to "make it their own." On the soundstage—especially in television—there's only one block-through before a rehearsal run-through, and then it's shot. It takes consistent concentration and the ability to set blocking quickly, especially when the actor is faced with matching the blocking hours or even days later.

In film, "hitting your marks" has a specific meaning. Onstage, an actor has a broad area of light in which to move. As long as he "finds his light," six inches to a foot either way won't alter the performance. The actor can change or turn and there isn't a problem—as long as he doesn't change anything to do with the pacing or the director's physical concept of the play. But in film and on television, if an actor misses his mark (a *T* marked on the floor with tape) by more than inch in a medium or close-up shot, he can expect to hear, "Cut!" which could cost the production company another thousand dollars.

Jane Alexander has said that for her, the most difficult aspect of filmwork is movement, or the restriction thereof. I enjoyed interviewing her because she was such a perfect test case; before her first film experience, her background was entirely stage. After starring on Broadway in *The Great White Hope*, she was cast in the film version with James Earl Jones. Her immediate response to my questions on the difference between stage and screen was that she felt extremely confined by the technical restrictions placed on her movements by the camera, specifically in medium and close-up shots. Because the cinematographer must be absolutely precise in his framing, focus, and lighting, Ms. Alexander felt completely restricted and missed the freedom of movement she so enjoys on stage. As time passed and experience followed, she learned to work well within the confines of the restrictions, but if asked today to cite the biggest difference between stage and screen, I think she would still say it is the freedom of movement.

Sound

Here's another screen element that actually helps the actor during filming. *Sound*. No projection! No overemphasis on articulation, enunciation, pronunciation, or vocal tricks. The actor has the freedom to allow only his thoughts and emotions to affect how he speaks. On the stage, every word counts and must be heard. After all, a theatrical-script is often literature. Roger Rees (*Nicholas Nickleby, Robin Hood: Men in Tights*, "Cheers") describes the screen experience, "You adapt your performance to different circumstances, but it's the technique that's different, not the actual acting . . . There's now a whole generation and a half of actors who only know about acting for the camera. But you're talking to a stage actor who has done some films; and it's harder for some-one who's done a lot of shouting in theatres, and a lot of lugging around of shields and furniture, to come in slightly under his energy." Many times while preparing a scene to shoot an actor might ask himself, "Can I do this line with a look?" which is a euphemism for Can it be done subtextually? Since the words are not the most important element, lines or ends of phrases are often thrown away or barely heard—it's very naturalistic.

The first thing the actor should do when reading a script is to throw away any punctuation. The screenwriter has to use punctuation so that anyone reading the script can understand what they are reading. But for the actor, punctuation should come out in the character's behavior. Just by thinking and feeling, the words will be motivated and the punctuation will follow. Oftentimes the words may come out run together, garbled, thrown away, or inaudible. A look will complete the sentence and sometimes carry more meaning than the words.

An actor can forget all sense of vocal projection in screen work. It's disconcerting for stage actors because it is ingrained in them to vocally "take stage" and create focus as they do with movement, performing something that people will want to watch. And they have all learned vocal tricks to help create that interest. On screen this is not done. As with movement, the camera and the editor create the focus. The actor must just *be*.

Choice Work

As we have seen, stage actors are used to rehearsal and plenty of personal preparation time to work out the various elements of their role in the play. By *elements* I mean the choices they are expected to make in terms of character, objectives, motivations, transitions, and so on. Many actors make those choices ahead of time and then confirm, reject, or modify them as rehearsals progress—agonizing over the most trivial details about their character and his actions.

In Lee Strasberg's master class when it was time to present a scene which the actor had painstakingly prepared for weeks, Lee expected minute, moment-to-moment preparation using, of course, "the Method." He assumed that the student had already gone through the appropriate number of sense memory exercis-es during preparation and rehearsal time. When the scene finished, the student would sit on the front of the stage and Lee would ask pointedly, "What did you try to do?" Whatever the student's answer, he would follow with, "How did you try to accomplish that?" The student would then proceed to describe all the wonderful exercises (private moment, overall, animal exercises, etc.) that led to the emotional truth of the scene. Lee would then tear apart the scene, piece by piece for forty-five minutes nonstop. And woe to the poor actor who hadn't prepared! (My ego is still a bit bruised by just such an experience.) But I remember and continue to admire the detail with which he could remember everything a student did. Lee expected his students to know what they were doing every moment on that stage. For him preparation was essential.

Because of the ever-changing nature of film work, the screen actor can never be sure of what to expect when he arrives on the set. Therefore, he must be able to throw out much, if not all, of his choice work preparation and be prepared to adjust to new information, even as his scene is being called. It's imperative to have the craft to make those changes abruptly and rapidly, internalizing and setting them, so as to be able to match them in the coverage.

Improvisation

In looking at the limitations of film and television, one finds little preparation, no time for rehearsal, and almost no direction. What does the actor do when a director changes everything at the last minute? Adjust! And what's another word for adjustment? Improvisation!

The very definition of improvisation—"To invent, to recite without preparation"—defines the major limitation of a screen actor. He has no time! Actors who are good at improvising—especially those who are used to being self-directed—have considerably fewer problems with the speed and pace of film and television than those who aren't. If direction is there, great. But if it isn't, you have to do it yourself. Knowing when something is working and how to make it work when it isn't, is the basis for what Lee Strasberg termed, "developing your own critical eye." This is an important skill to have when the pressure is building on a set; an actor's career may very well depend on it someday. And solid improvisation technique, training, and experience help create that critical eye.

Improvisation training is not only about the kind of comedy training you find at places like Second City, which is result-orientated for effect and comedy. That kind of experience stands on its own and is valuable, especially for sitcoms. The improvisation I am talking about is fundamental reality improvisation in which the actor creates motivated, believable new dialogue and/or physical business in an instant. Oftentimes directors will ask an actor to improvise all kinds of actions and dialogue in order to get into or out of a scene. Sitting at the bar on "Cheers," I would have to create a whole life for myself in order eventually to be at the right place at the right time for a particular line or group interaction.

But improvisation is also important when an actor must make adjustments quickly and then set them, being consistent and matching those adjustments through twenty takes and over hours of filming. By it's very nature, improvisation demands spontaneity. But as seen before, matching is a constant weight around the actors' neck, and while spontaneity and imagination are rewarded during the creative process, consistency and matching are what are needed during the technical process.

This can be the killer to creativity in film and television. All the spontaneous freshness— playing the moment—can go out the window with too many takes and too much repetition. What is left is a flat, imitative performance. (By the way, most directors understand this and they try to get the takes the first time if they can.)

Unfortunately, the technical needs of film production demand retakes. And the bigger the budget, the more retakes. The grapevine lists Michael Cimino's *Heaven's Gate* as having the record for most takes during the filming of a single scene—128. Imagine trying to keep that scene fresh for 128 takes!

Believability

After all the script work is done, after all the physical business is figured out, the final component that an actor brings to a performance is believability. Who you are, what your relationship is to the other characters in the scene, and what your objective is are important choices to make, but if you don't believe them, no one else will. On stage *or* on screen, believability is the one factor that is not an option. It's either there or it's not.

Believability is also the essential element in establishing *suspension of disbelief*. Without suspension of disbelief there's nothing to watch on the screen or stage except a bunch of yammering actors. When viewing any performance, intellectually you know that what you're watching is not actually taking place. Yet you are affected, sometimes to laughter, sometimes to tears. This happens because the writers, the director, the actors, and the craftsmen, through their collective talents, created a suspension of disbelief.

Imagine sitting in a darkened theatre. On the screen, Janet Leigh is being slashed to death in the famous shower scene from Hitchcock's *Psycho.* To this day, almost everyone who views that scene is affected by shock. What would happen if, just as the knife came down, a microphone dipped into the shot? The suspension of disbelief would immediately disappear. And that suspension can disappear just as fast with the actor's inability to believe. It is not a question of the *audience* believing what the actor is saying and doing. It is a question of the audience believing that the *actor* as the character believes what he is saying and doing. This is the foundation of suspension of disbelief.

In film and television, with constant starting and stopping for different angles and multiple takes, the actor must develop a facility for *instant believability*. It is essential to be able mentally to let go of the events of a scene, and go back to the beginning for a new start. Many stage actors begin their believability exercises several hours before curtain time, getting into their character and the events that will lead to the first scene of the first act. Film technique, with its need for repeatability and consistancy, requires a different approach.

Summary

So far I have been emphasizing broad areas of the acting craft that are most affected by the film medium. The next chapters will present a methodology to give a clearer view of the specific choices you must make to deal with the technical burdens film places on actors. It will be your choice where you practice your art, but if you want to establish a career in this industry you've got to understand the process and be prepared to meet it with a solid craft. By all means keep working in the theatre, but don't lose sight of the artistic and career-building possibilities that await you on the screen.

The Three-Level 3
System

Given a solid understanding of the technical and technique differences between stage and screen, it's time to confront the limitations that exist in film, thereby lessening their negative impact. Most actors, especially those of us working in television, have bemoaned the time factor at one point or another ("Boy, with a little more time, just one more rehearsal, this could have been better."). By the time most theatre actors are in their third or fourth week of performances, they have found a new and deeper understanding of their characters and their motivations. The pressure and insecurities of opening night are replaced by a confidence in the material and the ability to perform. The show evolves and becomes immensely more fulfilling and enjoyable. When working in film without these lead weeks of exploration, preparation, and performance, it quickly becomes obvious that the normal methodology for stage acting is not going to work. Bob Morgan, past head of the Boston University acting conservatory, put it unequivocally when he said, "The presumption that you can bring a performance [screen] immediately to the work is terrifying." Clearly, technique is needed that is more facile, more efficient, more specific, and just plain faster.

It has been my perception since I began studying theatre in the early sixties that the process of developing and preparing a role was often based on overintellectualization, rationalization, psychoanalysis, and a little mystification thrown in for effect. I remember a teacher who conducted acting class as if it were a group therapy session. (The scene from *Tootsie* where Dustin Hoffman argues his point on how to play a vegetable comes to mind as a classic example of the "method" on steroids.) The point is, in a month or so of rehearsal on stage, there is time for deep psychological exploration and a discussion of the finer motivations of character. But as we've already dicovered, in film and television there's barely enough time for the basics. And even if time were not a factor, given the communication skills of most directors, there would be no one on the set to discuss it with you.

Ellen Novack, casting director for the soap "One Life to Live," said in an *AFTRA* magazine interview, "We do in a day what other shows do in a week, and nobody has time to help you very much. You really have to fend for yourself. Theatre is very much about the acting process; the director has an interesting and creative [input] and something better comes out of it than what you saw in the audition. Unfortunately, soap operas are not really about process . . . in a soap actor, I need to get a sense that they will work for themselves, that they're not waiting for someone else to tell them what to do. There isn't time for a lot of process. The actor has to do that as homework."

The problem with home preparation is that once on the set, everything can change. So the emphasis of any preparation technique for film and television must address the need for speed and adaptability and the need to develop a high degree of technical craft.

In film and television the performance in each shot has to match. Every movement, every line, every action must match take after take. Marks have to be hit precisely. Step out of the key light, put a hat on your head on a different line, shift your weight to the wrong foot in a close-up and bump into the frame of the camera—hundreds of ways exist to force the director to say "Cut." (Sometimes a matching error gets so technical that it can go completely undetected by the director and is discovered only in the editing room.)

For example, John sits down close to Gertrude on his line, "I can't let you walk out of my life, Gertrude." "I must!" returns Gertrude as she dabs her eyes with her handkerchief. John leans over and wipes away one of her tears with his finger saying, "You and I are bound together, your tears are the fruit of your love for me."

This lovely yet so tragic scene could be shot from at least five different angles. If John were to lean in and wipe a tear away at a different time in each shot, the editor wouldn't be able to cut any of those angles together. The action wouldn't match, and he would be forced to use only the master (wide shot) or a two-shot. The fact that scenes are shot from multiple angles and the editor cuts these various shots into a completed scene means the actor must match his takes.

The physical restrictions imposed by tight camera angles and matching scenes can mean a major obstruction in freedom of movement and concentration for the film actor. The last thing an actor wants in her thoughts in the middle of a scene is, "On what word do I sit on the couch?" So a system of working that enables scenes to be matched necessitates a specific understanding and idea of where the actor is in the script and the scene at all times. Otherwise a beautifully played close-up may see only the editing-room floor.

Other elements exist in the scene besides the physical aspects of matching. These elements (thoughts and emotions) are the keys to the difference between the "performance" for the stage, and the "behavior" for the screen. That is why I developed the three-level system to help the actor successfully match all layers of her performance, without the performance becoming mechanical, predictable, and uninteresting.

What the audience assimilates as it watches a film is understood mainly from the visual language on the screen. What the actor does, says, thinks, and feels—what dictates the character's behavior—make up her visual language, and is how she communicates her choices to the audience. I have worked to incorporate these aspect of visual language into a system that is time-efficient, repeatable, and consistent.

To Act

In order to understand the nature of this screen technique, acting as an art form must be considered. First, however, it is necessary to understand the evolution of acting from its classical beginnings in Greece to the incorporation of screen acting during the twentieth century.

Historically, acting as a form or technique was practiced as a physical entity through voice and movement. Tommaso Salvini, the famous Italian actor from the 1800s, said, "The three requi-sites to play a great tragic role are voice, voice, and voice." From the Greeks wearing masks with megaphones in them, through the Roman spectacles, to the Italian Renaissance, the Elizabethan poeticism, the Comedie Francaise, and Italian commedia del' arte, acting was a purely external process, a physical exercise in storytelling. Real characters, real thoughts and emotions, and real behavior were not the goal. As Uta Hagen describes it in her book, *Respect for Acting*, "The Representational actor deliberately chooses to imitate or illustrate the character's behavior."

Since classicism, acting moved toward the concept of real-ism, and definitions of what it is "to act" abound. Diderot, in his *Paradox* (as described by Harold Clurman of Group Theater fame), set forth that "genuine emotion experienced during the actor's exercise of this art impedes esthetic truth and effectiveness." Uta Hagen writes, "The actor attempts to reveal human behavior through a use of himself, through an understanding of himself and consequently an understanding of the character he is por-traying . . . the actor trusts that a form will result from identification with the character and the discovery of his charac-ter's actions, and works on stage for a moment-to-moment sub-jective experience." Robert Lewis offers this definition: "that basic technique of talking and listening with intention, experiencing the truth of the moment." Even Peter O'Toole commented, "I real-ly don't know what it is. I learn my lines, change shape and get on with it."

Now it's my turn. My definition of acting is . . . *to be*. To be (I am). Simple, accurate, specific, and directed at bringing the char-acter's emotional truth and true behavior onto the screen: *I am*. In film, the camera records images of behavior that tell the story. The actor's sole responsibility is to create motivated behavior—consistently—and leave the technical details to others. The script and the director give the outline, or gross description, of the char-acter's behavior; the actor provides the details. Once these details, or *choices*, are made, the actor becomes the character and then behaves as her character would in the given set of circum-stances. It shouldn't be any more complicated than that. I want it to be that elemental and simplistic.

The model I have constructed for my three-level system is taken directly from my understanding of psychology, human observation, and personal experience in working with more than one thousand actors over a period of thirty years, acting, directing, teaching, and learning.

LEVEL 1: Behavior (physical)
Level one is the physical level—the behavior of the character; what the character says and does.

LEVEL 2: Subtext
Level two is subtext—the thought motivation behind the character's behavior; what the character is thinking from moment to moment.

LEVEL 3: Emotions
Level three is the emotional motivation of the character's behavior; what the character is feeling moment to moment.

Level 1: Behavior (Physical)

The art of the screen actor is in creating the behavior of a real character. The first element of the three-level system, which ultimately becomes the final result of the second and third, is therefore behavior or the physical level—physical because it is what is physically recorded. It is empirical. It exists visually on film and audibly on tape. It is recorded as images with sound on film or videotape and those images tell the story in visual language. Behavior is defined as what the character says and does. The screenwriter gives us the lines and a general description of the actions, and the director gives us the specific actions through blocking—a kind of road map for the actor. It is up to the actor to create real believable behavior from those static elements. Levels two and three create the motivation for that behavior.

But level one has another component. It also encompasses the technical range of screen expertise: knowing your way around the set; how to hit marks; what each camera angle looks like; what you physically can or can not do on a given shot; and how to remember what you do physically so that your takes match. A screen actor needs to have a good command of this aspect of film craft and good control of the physical level.

The problem is that some actors, especially in television, stop at level-one technique and consider it good acting. If they can walk, talk, and chew gum with a moderate degree of realism or naturalism, they consider themselves actors. Behavior becomes a technique unto itself—impersonated and implied. And behavior that is unmotivated and unjustified is imitative. With no substantive layers of motivation, no subtext, no real emotions, we're watching a conversation with attitudes. It is very interesting that there is a much higher degree of expectation of the actor in film, whereas sadly, we settle for so much less in television.

Of course, there are many fine actors in the television industry and, conversely, there are film actors, even huge "stars" bringing in millions in box-office dollars, who are completely external, mechanical actors (Arnold Schwartzenegger, Jean-Claude Van Damme, Chuck Norris, etc.). As a producer, however, you would love to have Arnold Schwartzenegger star in your movie because statistics say you would make a lot of money. Is he a great or even a good actor? Actually, the answer doesn't have anything to do with why his films make money or why they are even entertaining. By playing the right character in the right genre of film, even Arnold has enough level-one craft to produce a performance that works for the piece. The point is, you should want to be able to do much more.

Even under normal screen conditions, the actor is sometimes faced with pressure situations where she's just trying to survive—hoping she gets her lines right and hits her marks. That's where level-one craft is of great value. But merely getting by with good level-one work is not enough if you are a serious actor. You wouldn't accept this type of performance on the stage and you shouldn't accept it on the screen.

In order to able to produce and reproduce true behavior on demand, we need to support that behavior with motivation. What motivates you or I to behave as we do? We think and we feel. It's as simple as that. How we think and feel motivates what we say and do. Those are the only two elements the actor has available to create motivated behavior.

Level 2: Subtext

Stanislavsky was thought to be the first acting theorist to avail himself of the science of psychology to determine the motivation of behavior. He once said, "I am simply trying to put down something which is based on the laws of creation." His interest in realism brought him to the psychology guru of the day, Pavlov.

Modern day psychologists, whether behaviorists, cognitive theorists, Freudians, or Jungians, all have their own specific approaches to human behavior. In college psychology courses we learn that man is ruled by the id, the ego, and the superego. My concept doesn't argue the differences in cognitive/behavioral theory; it tends to coalesce and simplify them.

Everyone agrees that human beings think and that how and what they think is a major factor in determining their behavior. As Descartes said, "I think, therefore I am." We have learned that film and television are subtextual mediums. The camera sees through the eyes and reads thought. The audience watching a play cannot see the actor's eyes much less see what's in them. So it is important that an actor understand how essentially subtext separates stage from screen performance. Now, I'm not a heretic saying there is no subtext in stage acting. Of course there is. In the theatre I use it constantly, both as an actor and as a director. But the writing establishes the subtext in theatre, and the subtlety of what the actor can communicate through subtext is nowhere near as viable as it is in film.

Because film is so subtextual, scenes are written so that what a character says and does is not always what is actually happening—it is the thinking that makes the difference. Actors have to look at the script and understand the whole scene may be played subtextually; in other words—it isn't in the writing, it isn't in the words. Audiences aren't there to listen to what the character is saying, they are there to see what she is really saying, underneath the words and actions. That is what makes a performance fascinating and compelling to watch.

Subtext is part of our everyday behavior. For instance, idiomatic expressions come about when a consistent use of subtext is universally understood; expressions like "get off my back" or "what a piece of work" received their eventual meanings through an evolution of subtext. Just because one says, "Hi, how are you? Nice to see you," doesn't mean that one necessarily thinks or feels that way. Many different connotations and meanings could derive from that statement depending on the thoughts of the person saying it.

Everyone uses this kind of day-to-day communication, intending our subtext to be read. Sometimes, though, we want to keep our subtext private. Often we will cover our thoughts with the physical level. For instance, you might find yourself saying to a perfectly obnoxious person, "Hi, Bill. Nice to see you" when in actuality you are thinking, "What is this jerk doing here?" In a social situation, you would edit your private thoughts and not say what you're thinking. But those inner thoughts are there and the camera picks them up. So it matters greatly what thoughts are in an actor's head whenever she says something on film. The question has always had a chicken-and-egg analogy to it; some say you give meaning to a line through physical manipulation using intonation and emphasis, while others believe the thought motivates what eventually becomes the character's verbal expression. My choice is obvious.

Be a people watcher. Watch how they behave and react to life happening around them—watch their minds at work. Watch politicians at a news conference—they are masters at hiding their thoughts. Watch people who are insensitive or tactless—they don't edit their thoughts; whatever they think finds its way to their mouth.

Thoughts are always behind what a character is saying. But clearly there are also thoughts going on when a character is not saying anything—when she is just listening, or no one is talking, or she's in a scene by herself. One of the most important parts of filmmaking, and the element in film that tells the greatest story by visual means is the reaction shot. Remember the old truism, "Acting is reacting"? How a character reacts to what another character says will reveal more about her character and the plot than almost any line she could say. And reaction shots depend on listening. Some acting teachers consider listening to be *the* most important element to the actor's craft. Listening defines not only *hearing* but also *sensing* perceptions intuitively from another person.

In my observations, I have found there are four "stages" to the listening process that can be picked up by the camera.

1. *Hearing*—Jim hears his friend Anne say, "Do you want my tickets to the playoffs tonight? I gotta go out of town on business." Before Jim even understands what the words mean, there is an instant of pure listening—Jim just heard words. Another example would be a conversation in which something is said out of context, and there is a brief moment when the listener hasn't followed the course of the conversation. That's hearing words without understanding.

2. *Understanding* - Jim's mind makes the connection and understands what Anne is saying; i.e., Jim comprehends that he is possibly going to be able to go to the game because Anne can't.

3. *Internal Reaction* - Jim reacts to what he now understands subtextually and emotionally. He might think, " The Lakers and Celtics! Fabulous! What an unlucky break for poor Anne."

4. *External Expression* - Those thoughts and emotions motivate an external response. Sometimes it can be so subtle that nothing seems to be there. In this case it might be, "Sorry you can't go but I'd love to!" Or Jim might give a whooping yell and give Anne a bear hug.

I have experimented many times on and off camera watching for those four stages. Sometimes the action and reaction happen so quickly that all four stages blend together. At other times, amazingly long moments occur between stages. One of my favorite classroom exercises has been to seat a student in front of me so that the class can observe the same things I do. (I am also videotaping the student using a close-up.)

I begin a normal conversation with the student asking her such questions as Where are you from? and What do your parents do?—questions which allow her to relax as though in a normal conversation. I then might ask a question like, "Describe the house you grew up in." Without fail, the student's eyes look off in a number of directions as she visually sees the house she grew up in (visual subtext). Then, having established one direction with the conversation, I will take a complete change of direction: "When did your father beat you last?" or "Do you wear red under-wear?"—saying anything that catches the student unawares.

The reaction is all there. Reviewing the tape the class is usually able to see each listening stage quite distinctly. And if they happen too quickly and run together, I slow down the tape to isolate each moment. In an actual scene, however, actors sometimes run into problems because they know the script so well they will *anticipate* reactions to events and the listening is lost. On stage, actors are certainly required to listen, but the audience couldn't possibly see any of the subtleties that are the stock-in-trade of film. They only see and hear Anne ask the question and then see and hear Jim's final reaction. Madeline Kahn, no stranger to stage or screen, said in *Conversations in the Wings*, "On stage your method of transmitting the material is more active. You are the transmitter. . . . Since you are the mechanical means by which the message is sent out—rather than a camera picking it up—you use your whole physical self in addition to the truth of the character." On screen, the camera is right there, watching the face like a hawk, reading everything.

This is subtext. And the definition of subtext is self-explanatory: *sub*, meaning *under* and *text* meaning *the written word*. It is *any* thought that the character has, from overt thoughts that are clearly in the conscious mind motivating an actual line and that can be said almost out loud, to subtle, layered thoughts deep in the subconscious, nagging at the character. The more proficient an actor is, the more layered (subtextually) a performance can be. And the more conflicting thoughts that are occurring within the character at the same moment, the more fascinating the performance. Holly Hunter's work in *The Piano* integrated an incredible range of contradictory, layered thoughts which the camera read beautifully.

The concept of a subtext is part of many acting theories, while various techniques integrate subtext by the use of "intentions." Robert Lewis in *Advice to the Players* combines objectives and subtext when he writes, "I believe an intention is the most important element of the acting craft. Some call this element of the craft 'objective.' Others refer to it as the inner-action . . . still others simply say it's the subtext." He later wrote of the late Dame Edith Evans, "she always asked to have her part typed out with a blank space under each line. And in that space she wrote what she called her 'unspoken part.' She put underneath the lines what she meant by what she said—her thoughts—her intentions." Later he defines it as, "Intention is what you are really doing on the stage at any given moment, regardless of what you are saying, if it's a silent scene or if you are listening. . . . It is in fact, your reason for being on the stage."

Although thoughts are fleeting and ephemeral, the subtextual level still needs to be matched on each take. If an actor on camera is thinking one thing in a two-shot, and the editor cuts to a close-up of him with a different thought, even though everything is the same physically, it becomes a *different* performance, and the two pieces of film won't match.

On stage, of course, there are no problems with "playing the moment," that is, keeping things spontaneous even though the performance is slightly different from one night to the next. But in film this can be a problem. Not matching subtextually is an understated mistake most laymen would have trouble detecting. Even some directors have the same lack of perception. But control over this level separates an actor who is a craftsman from an actor who is a journeyman.

Mr. Lewis combines objectives and subtext together to form intentions. Actors tend to generalize when they use intentions for entire beats (sections) of a scene. Since the actor doesn't know which small moment out of the whole scene the director might use as a close-up, she needs to be much more specific than just what her intentions are, in a given beat of a scene, in order to match her takes. That is why I break the scene down to a much more specific structure to follow what the character is thinking and feeling. A "through line" must be sustained every moment the actor is on the screen for every camera angle, every take. In the next chapter these objectives (intentions) are examined more closely in order to see how all the choices affect the subtextual level.

CHARACTER TRUTH VERSUS PERSONAL TRUTH

Now let's interject the element of character in this discussion on subtext and focus on how a *character* would behave in a given situation versus how *you* (the actor) would behave in that same situation. If you would *not* behave the same way as the character, then you must use *character truth*. If, on the other hand, you *would* respond the same way, then you can use *personal truth*.

Obviously it is much easier to play someone who thinks and feels exactly like you do. Take, for example, Charles Manson, whose thought pattern would be different than, say, Ronald Reagan. In playing a character like Manson, a deranged, cold-blooded, psychopathic killer, the actor has a lot of work to do—not only in level one, how the character walks and talks, but also in level two, how he thinks. What strange images and convoluted thoughts must a brain like that produce? What thought patterns? Many people think that Charles Manson behaves as he does deliberately, knowing he's provoking and inciting people, that his actual thinking is completely different from what he is saying, and that he speaks as part of a character he is playing. Watch Manson on a television interview sometime. It's difficult to know exactly how much is a show.

Anthony Hopkins' character in *The Silence of the Lambs* comes to mind. The character's truth came from his performance. Dr. Lecter's behavior clearly came from a considerably different subtextual line than Hopkins's character in *The Remains of the Day*. Whatever choice an actor eventually makes for his character, it is important to understand that personal truth and character truth are known and realized only by that actor. Obviously personal truth is dictated by the actor's life, upbringing, education, friends, family, a plethora of life experiences. My personal truth may be quite different than another actor's, and those differences in thoughts show up on screen as indices of character. Only *you* have the specific thought patterns that you do and these thought patterns motivate your behavior.

When playing character truth, an actor has to shift into another thought pattern. The further away the character's truth is from the actor's personal truth, the more difficult it is to create motivated behavior, especially in film. Exaggeration, impersonation, and playing caricatures show up pathetically on screen. That is why character range strongly defines an actor's talent and ability. It seems obvious that Schwarzenegger's character range is limited, whereas De Niro, Hoffman, Streep, or Pacino have an almost limitless range. As much as people try to put those actors into a category (because they are stars), another role will come along and another character will emerge from their arsenal. In the old "studio" days, stars like Clark Gable and John Wayne weren't allowed to play anything that wasn't true to their screen personas. The contract star system is long gone, and today's stars are on their own to choose the characters they play.

THE NATURE OF THOUGHTS

Whether the actor is thinking character thoughts or personal thoughts, those thoughts are private—and unedited. People know they can cover their thoughts up, especially when they don't want anybody else to see them. I can watch an attractive person walk down the street, think the most outrageous things, and visualize the most interesting scenarios with the most mundane expression on my face. It is normal to free-associate.

The point is that thoughts are not a bunch of words running around in the brain. They consist of electrical impulses. When we try to translate those impulses into words, they tend to sound like lines we say to ourselves, much like characters in a Woody Allen film sitting around the table, each expressing their thoughts. But some of our thoughts come to us as visual imagery. Listening to a musical performance, for instance, can evoke beautiful images in our mind. Or if I ask an actor to describe her house, and she replies, "Well, it's a white clapboard house on a hill with these orange shutters and grass—it grows right up to some apple trees that hang over my back fence," I can watch her recall and visualize a picture of her house as she describes it. That is subtext too, a visual thought process going on in the mind.

There is also a verbal form of thought processes. For example, I might say to a loved one, "I'd really like to see you tonight . . ." And my thoughts might range anywhere from, "God, I miss you. You're everything I think about" to "I wonder if it's still raining? I don't want to go over there if it's wet outside." But subtextual choices are not invented in a vacuum; they depend greatly on many other choices that will be considered in the next chapter.

Consider why it is important for an actor to know what her subtext is in relation to matching takes. If, in the master shot, the character is thinking, "I'm losing you and I miss you so terribly. I've got to see you," and in the close-up she is thinking, "Don't you love me anymore, why don't you want to see me?" the resulting behavior from the actor's character will appear on the screen quite differently and will affect the line itself and every line that comes after it. If the editor wants to cut a close-up in that master shot and the actor's subtext differs, two different performances will be recorded and they won't match. Sometimes in television, where there is much less time available and, therefore, fewer shots from which the editor can choose, edited sequences are aired with different performances going on in different shots. Start watching television from a more technical view and see what you can pick up.

If the actor is truly in the subtextual level in her performance in front of the camera—if she is thinking like the character moment to moment—then her behavior will be motivated. If she knows where her marks are, knows her lines perfectly, has her blocking set, and is confident with her craft, then all the actor has to do is trust and let the behavior happen. Once the preparation is over, the only thing on the actor's mind should be the character's thoughts. From the moment the director says, "Action!" to the moment he says, "Cut!" the actor cannot be thinking, "How many steps do I take here?" or "What is my next line?" or "I gotta make sure I get my chin up in the correct position for that particular light source over there." There must be a throughline of subtext that has to be the number one priority when actually shooting. If the actor suddenly gets desperate and thinks, "God, I should have been two steps over." or "I'm gonna be late for that mark," the camera will see it. When actors are prepared and finally trust that they will think as the character does, they experience a great sense of release from the technical restrictions and the freedom to truly *be* that character.

Level 3: Emotions

Now we come to the very heart of the performance—the third or *emotional* level. Like Stanislavsky and Strasberg, I believe that without a true, full emotional investment, the rest is unmotivated, physical, imitative performing. Very simply: the emotional level is defined as what the character is feeling. In this three-level system, what the character thinks and feels motivates what the character says and does (behavior); in other words, levels two and three motivate the first level—the physical (behavior). It always comes back to behavior because behavior is what is filmed.

In real life people don't usually know what they're going to do or say before they say or do it: behavior is mostly spontaneous. And so should acting be. But as actors, we also must satisfy our craft, and that means consistent, repeatable spontaneity. The trouble is, the acting process is the reverse of real life; we are told what to do by the director, told what to say by the writer. The actor's job is to turn this process around. The preparation work is filling out details and making choices about levels two and three—what the character is thinking and feeling. Those choices have to be internalized and set so that when we get into the performance mode, the character's behavior remains consistent no matter how many takes there are. The takes will match because the thinking and feeling are the same every time and therefore what the character says and does will be the same. Obviously this is not an exact science, and the actor could never expect to think and feel exactly the same things every time, but the goal should be consistent and repeatable behavior.

What happens to many stage actors while shooting a master shot is that even though they are totally involved in their character's emotional level, the master is shot at 7:30 in the morning and along about 2:00 or 3:00 in the afternoon they are asked to match a section of the scene in a close-up. The director tells the actor, "We're going to skip to the middle of your major speech here and start from where you pick up the gun. Just turn on the same mark as you did in the master and start your line as you turn. That's all I want." Unfortunately, the inexperienced actor has no idea what she did seven hours ago in the master shot. She may well remember what her line and blocking were at the time, but as to the specifics of her emotions, she hasn't a clue. In this situation the actor tends simply to imitate what she did in the master or create something that works at the moment. Consequently, the character's behavior seven hours later will appear different from that of seven hours earlier. And the editor will not be a happy camper.

A credible and repeatable performance, therefore, begins with this very important emotional layer. Two distinct parts of this layer are of particular importance to the film actor.

DEFINING THE EMOTIONAL TONE

Rarely do people feel just one emotion at any given moment. Emotions are more complex than that. There are layers of emotional tones; some are of a similar nature (anger, frustration, resentment) and some are in conflict but exist in the same moment (love, anxiety, hostility, excitement). The better the actor, the better the control of the emotions and the greater the range of emotions. For example, De Niro's characterization of LaMotta in *Raging Bull* demonstrated a powerful and revealing display of emotional layering. A lesser actor would have played LaMotta as a violent, brutal, frustrated individual. But look at some of De Niro's scenes; there is an amazing combination of anger, frustration, love, pain, hurt, rejection, fear, and jealousy— all going on at the same time. It is almost as if there are little sparks of intensity of one emotion or another rising up, jabbing at him, and forcing him into an incredible variety of mercurial behavior, from beating up his wife to breaking down in tears. Very few actors could even approach the expanse and depth of emotion that De Niro expressed in that performance, which not surprisingly was recognized by his peers and won him an Academy Award.

The control over emotional layering derives from the actor's ability to define the emotional tone of his character, moment to moment. The actor must go though each scene of the script, moment to moment, and make decisions about what is happening to the character emotionally. As the title of this book implies, actors make choices. And these choices create the performance. It cannot be dictated by "whatever happens, happens . . . I'm gonna play the now, I'm gonna play the moment—whatever I feel, I feel." That kind of attitude can have unfortunate consequences.

But the ability to make choices and to adjust emotionally, given the limitation of time in film, implies that an actor has the craft to make those adjustments and make them quickly. If the choice doesn't work or the director wants something else, she adjusts and makes another choice. It can be a problem for actors who don't have the training or experience to deal with the emotional level. They lack control, and they rely on inspiration or moment-to-moment playing to create the emotions of the character. In film, actors need the ability to make a choice, play that choice, then repeat that choice twenty takes in a row. Actors with good craft can do that.

EMOTIONAL INTENSITY

The second element of the emotional level is *intensity*. After defining the emotional tone, you have to realize the intensity of each of those emotions. If the character is feeling fear, rejection, love, hate—all at the same time—that's all well and good, but what is the intensity of these emotions? And when does that intensity change from moment to moment? These changes create sometimes dramatic changes in the character's behavior. We are dealing with very subtle nuances of an actor's performance that clearly are experienced in the stage actor's craft as well. But the screen actor must always be aware of the special technical needs of the profession when dealing with the emotional level: no time, little rehearsal, and matching.

Choosing the wrong intensity for an emotion can be as damaging as playing the wrong emotion itself. There is a particular trap that many actors fall prey to: overemotional acting. Lee Strasberg continually berated actors who were working with the Method and confused emotional truth with emotional excess. In a master class, he once tore an actor's performance apart, reducing her to tears because she was so heavy on her emotional choices. He demanded control and restraint.

Many times the wrong intensity causes "over-the-top" acting or "soap-opera acting." The emotional choices are too intense for a particular moment, not necessarily because the actor isn't really feeling the emotions or that the chosen emotions aren't right for the moment, but only that they were too intense. Soaps are exceptionally susceptible to intensity transgressions because of the emphasis placed on emotions in order to create the drama. Remember, soaps are shot in one day on one soundstage with little or no action to create interest. They rely on "talking heads" and page after page of nothing but dialogue. And as we've already discussed, all dialogue and no action breeds boredom. Hence the need for strong characters who have strong needs that result in strong emotions. The trick is to choose the right emotion with the right intensity and not cross the line.

Emotions then, are not the problem; control is. Matching also rears its ugly head once again. The different emotions (the emotional layering) *and* the intensity of those emotions must match. In a master where the character is in an argument with her boss over a raise, the character feels frustration with a little anger and resentment involved. Hours later a close-up is shot and it's the actor's moment to shine. The blood is pumping and the adrenaline is racing. She finds herself getting more intensely emotional about the scene than she was in the master. Days later, when the editor wants to cut from the master to the close-up right in the middle of the great moment, she won't be able to. The film won't match. It may be true that the same words, the same actions, and the same thoughts are used, but it won't match if the emotional intensity is not consistent. As Michael Caine aptly put it, "It's your job to remember the emotional nature of the master in complete detail." Be aware, though, that the director might want something different on different takes of a close-up. Many times a director will cover his options—after the actor has a good take in the can—if he feels a certain moment might work better with a different emotional cast to it. That is his option; the actor's job is to adjust.

Emotional adjustments in film and television are particularly worrisome. Once the actor gets on the set and plays a scene as he's prepared it, a director's change of the character's emotions can be unnerving, especially if the actor is dependent on emotional preparation. The director may say, "I see you're playing anger and frustration—it's too heavy for me. I want annoyance and frustration and no anger—plus a little sarcasm and condescension, rather than anger—just more annoyance and frustration." Then she yells, "Okay. First positions! Let's shoot it." There has been no time for rehearsal, no time to go back to the trailer and do some sense memory exercise to get that emotion. The actor has to give it to the director right there. Then, of course, if she likes it, the director will shoot it and maybe a few other angles as well that the actor will have to match hours or days later. This clearly necessitates good control—the ability to create the emotional truth and then to be able to set it and reproduce it at will. Things change very fast on a film set; actors have to adjust just as quickly.

These then, are the three levels: the physical (behavior), the subtextual, and the emotional. What you think and feel motivates what you say and do. It may seem complicated in theory but quickly becomes second nature in practice. Most of you already are used to thinking and feeling like the character on stage. So much so that when you don't, you feel empty, as if something were missing. That inner connection becomes an integral step in "developing your own critical eye." Remember, in film and television you have to be able to be self-directed. Knowing you are thinking and feeling as the character is the first criterion in knowing whether you're "in" (character and believability) or "out" in relation to that critical eye. When you're "out" you often have to make the adjustments consciously. But the three-level system is a technique—a guide or a means, not an end in itself. Just as in any learned motor skill, technique is a process that helps you learn a repeatable event. In golf, when you've learned a complicated technique to swing a club, you don't dwell on the elements of the technique as you swing, you just swing the club. If you've got the technique right (hands here, weight there, etc.) the ball goes straight down the fairway. If not, the ball goes into the woods. As Martha Graham said about technique, "It frees the spirit." The three-level system is meant to do the same thing for acting; it allows you to free the spirit of your character and just *be.*

It's very similar to learning a language. There comes a point— a step—when translating English into French—before beginning and actually thinking and effortlessly speaking in French: you have to trust that it will happen. This is very similar to what I am talking about here. You finally trust that during the actual scene all you have to do is think and feel. Those lines will be there, you'll hit your marks, you'll be able to listen and react, and your behavior will be consistent because you're prepared and because your technique is solid. Doubt kills the life of the character. Make a choice and trust it.

My definition of acting is *I am* or *to be*—therefore you are the character. If you are playing a district attorney, it's not because you can do an impersonation that looks and sounds like her, but because you can think and feel like her. Actors use many different keys to unlock a character. De Niro decided he needed to gain fifty pounds to play Jake LaMotta correctly, and he put the weight on himself rather than rely on latex, padding, or makeup. Other actors might have done things differently. There is no point in criticizing somebody for the way they work; either you are the character or you are imitating.

There is an often-told story of Dustin Hoffman and Sir Laurence Olivier in *Marathon Man.* During a critical scene, Dustin Hoffman was preparing in his methodological way, and the action called for him to have run a great distance and be all out of breath. Once they got ready to shoot, Hoffman was reported to have said,

"Get everything ready, I'm gonna run, when I get back have the cameras rolling." He went out, ran, came back, jumped into place, and the director yelled, "Action!" When they were about to shoot another take, Mr. Hoffman again requested time to run. Olivier interjected, "My dear fellow, why don't you try acting?"

I've heard the story told differently many times, but the essential elements are consistent and serve to illustrate differences in working methods. The English supposedly work from the outside in, Hoffman and Streep clearly like to work from the inside out. I've taken a particular stance in my work with the three-level system—working from the inside out. I also believe that however Olivier got to his character, once he was the character, he felt and thought like the character.

It is also the juxtaposition of these three layers that creates the nuances of a performance. Let's look at an example:

> **Level one**—*behavior*. A man touches a woman's cheek very lightly and says, "I love you."
> **Level two**—*subtext*. "I love you, darling."
> **Level three**—*emotions*. He's feeling love, affection, caring, tenderness, joy, and excitement.

That would be a straightforward interpretation of the line and the scene. Let's look at another, slightly different relationship between the two characters. Let's make the choice that the man does indeed love the woman, but he is insecure about that love and the relationship itself. He has low self-esteem and a poor self-image and doesn't trust that she loves him enough. How will this affect the three levels? Let's look at them. He's still sitting there, he still reaches over and brushes her cheek, but now the behavior will be more tentative. Although he says the exact same thing and is directed to do the exact same physical gesture, the behavior will be different because it is motivated differently by different subtext and emotions.

> **Level one**—*behavior*. The man touches the woman's cheek very lightly and says, "I love you."
> **Level two**—*subtext*. Perhaps his thoughts are now, "My God, I love you. If you could only love me as much."
> **Level three**—*emotions*. Certainly he's feeling love and caring and tenderness, but what else? Now there is insecurity, fear, a little frustration, maybe even a little rejection and hurt.

And we have a completely different moment. His behavior comes from his thoughts and feelings about her, but now his thoughts conflict with his emotions. The juxtaposition of loving thoughts with feelings of insecurity create a conflict, and that is interesting. He will smile and say those lines tenderly, but the very gesture of brushing her cheek with tentativeness will speak absolute volumes. If the actor tries to impose that behavior on the physical level, without thinking and feeling those things, the performance will become mechanical rather than emotionally truthful.

As you can see, the ultimate choice of how the line is translated into behavior depends on all the actor's other choices, i.e., character, relationships, object, etc. Every choice can change the behavior.

One more: The man has been friends with the girl for years and only feels affection for her. The man's behavior is withdrawn and halting. He probably reaches to touch her in an affectionate gesture, but the guilt and remorse holds him back.

> **Level one**—*behavior.* The man touches the woman's cheek and says, "I love you."
> **Level two**—*subtext.* "She's a terrific girl, I wish I could really love her."
> **Level three**—*emotions.* He's feeling affection, caring, remorse, guilt, and a little loss.

If you looked at five of Schwarzenegger's love scenes from five of his movies, you'd probably see the exact same behavior in each one—with a possible exception when he played a robot. He is good at playing emotionless characters. Then take a look at five love scenes from Meryl Streep's films, or any actor you consider to be a quality actor.

The three-level system also helps alleviate the problem of staleness when matching takes over a long period of time. How does an actor keep something fresh, take after take? As an example, try to say elephant fifty times fast.

Done? Very soon—perhaps by the tenth or eleventh time you said the word—*elephant* became something else—it probably sounded similar to *benalavant*. The reason this happens is that you are just saying a word. Now try the exercise over again but this time, while you say the word, have a mental picture of a large African elephant, a subtextual image of this huge beast with its trunk raised in the air, its ears flapping back, its tusks gleaming in the sunlight (with one of them broken off a bit at the tip). Have that mental, visual, subtextual image in your mind while you say, "elephant." Except for a tired tongue, elephant stays elephant every time.

And that is how a scene is done—from six or seven different set-ups with a couple of master shots, several two-shots, over-the-shoulders, cutaways, singles, extreme close-ups, and tight close-ups with two, three, or five takes from each one of those camera angles, over a five-hour time span. With every take the director wants to shoot in a close-up, no matter how small a segment, your behavior will be the same each time and your takes will match if the three levels are there. What's more, the performance will be fresh, believable, and motivated every single time because it won't be an imitative performance, it will be motivated behavior.

One of the main reasons for this system, besides the technical aspects of speed and efficiency, is that it de-intellectualizes and de-rationalizes the process. Now you can see why this system cuts to the absolute basic core of the actor's work: "What am I thinking and feeling and therefore what is my behavior in this scene?" In making those decisions about what the character will think and feel, the actor has to answer these important questions: Who am I? Who is the other person in the scene? What do I want? This information is then translated into specific, definite choices that create action or "doing" rather than intellectualizing.

When you receive that script late at night and are expected to be on the set the next morning, you will now be able to look closely at the scene, ask questions, and make choices based on the answers to those questions. On the set the next day, when the director puts you on your mark, tells you your blocking, and then runs the scene, you will have concrete, active choices to rely on. Then as you listen to the director's criticism and listen to the other actors' choices (they may give a completely different kind of emotional response than expected) you can adjust your choices quickly and efficiently. You can go back to the script and say, "Aha! Here I thought she would be much more understanding and sensitive to my character, but I'm getting much more aggression." You can go back and restructure your choices according to the new information. When it's time to film you already will have set what you are going to do. It may be hours or days later, but if they want to pick up (redo) any part of that scene, you can go back and know what you were thinking and feeling—and therefore consistently replicate your character's actions and behavior.

Six Choices 4

Because the three-level system is elemental in nature, you can now recognize how this technique helps you overcome the limitations of the film medium. With lack of time, little or no preparation, limited if any rehearsals, and often no constructive feedback from the director, you as a film actor need a system that is facile and efficient and one that can be relied upon to carry you through technically long and often brutal shooting schedules.

I have two specific reasons for calling this book *The Actor's Choice*. The first is the assumption that as an actor, it should ultimately be your choice to work in any medium available to you. Whether you pursue a career in film, television, commercials, theatre, or any combination, the choice should be up to you—provided you have developed the craft to do so.

The second reason has to do with the actual choices an actor makes to determine his performance. It has always been my contention that the actor's talent or art is defined by the ability to make and play great choices. In all other art forms, greatness is derived from the artist's ability to express great ideas. Picasso and Bach possessed great craft, but they also had a great vision to reveal to the world. For the actor, it is through his choices that we perceive his vision. And for the most accomplished actors, it is their character range and emotional range that distinguish their true talent. Where, during the "studio days," movie stars were forced to play only a limited range of character as defined by their "on-screen personality," today's actor completely rejects limitations as to character range. For most, it is a point of artistic honor to constantly expand that range. This chapter explores all the choices and explains how the screen actor prepares those choices for a performance on film.

How does this three-level system relate to the choices the actor must make in order to create the specificity needed in film?

The ability to get any role and then to play that role successfully comes down to an ability as an actor to make a choice, play it, and ultimately see that choice on the screen. The better the choices he makes (active and interesting), the more likely he will be to get the part and the better his ultimate performance will be.

What kind of choices? I have detailed six choices that are fundamental to any scene an actor will audition for or play. As with the three-level concept, I again have leaned toward being specific, efficient, and elemental with emphasis on consistency and repeatability because of the time and technical demands of the medium. I want to remove as much overintellectualization and rationalization as possible. There is no time to agonize over what the character had for breakfast when there is only twenty minutes to prepare for an audition. But it is also imperative that the actor make specific, active choices in the time available rather than generic or clichéd ones. In my approach to preparation, there is an important sequential nature to choice work.

The remarkable truth about the acting process is that if twenty actors of similar age and type all played Hamlet in the same production, one would see a very different Hamlet in each performance. It is fascinating to watch the many consistent and divergent moments of the performances of Laurence Olivier, Richard Burton, and Mel Gibson in their respective portrayals of the brooding Dane. The reason for the divergence is that each actor makes different major or subtle choices given their own preferences, background, and training.

As in the theatre, the text is the starting place, and because the individual scene is the basic component of any script, the scene initiates our choices. In order to illustrate the process of selecting the six choices, I have written a scene formatted in a conventional film and television style. Throughout the coming sections, I will refer to this sample scene. You should always be looking for *your* choices, whether you could play Bill or Beth. For brevity's sake I will look primarily at Bill's choices. The examples I use will not necessarily be *the* choice. There is no *one* choice; ultimately, there is only *your* choice.

FADE IN

43 INT. APARTMENT - KITCHEN - EVENING   43

> BETH DUNNE, *an attractive thirty-five-year-old advertising-account executive is busy preparing dinner. She is strong willed, very competent, successful, and is home late from her office and quickly throwing a meal together. She grabs for a heated pot on the stove and reacts as she feels the pain.*

>   BETH
>   Damn it!

> BETH *drops the pot and goes to the refrigerator to put ice on the burn.*

44 INT. APARTMENT - LIVING ROOM   44

> BILL DUNNE, *athletic, good looking, forty-five year old lawyer enters through the front door, wearily crosses to the table behind the sofa, puts his briefcase down, takes off his suit coat and absentmindedly leafs through the mail.*

>   BETH
>   *(from kitchen)*
>   Is that you Bill?

>   BILL
>   Yeah, I'm home.

> BILL *drops the mail and heads for the kitchen.*

>   BILL *(cont.)*
>   Did you get some more bourbon?

45 INT. KITCHEN   45

BILL *enters and heads for the liquor cabinet.*

> BETH
> It's on the counter. I'm late, fix it
> yourself will you?. . . You look tired.
> That kind of a day?

BILL *opens refrigerator to get ice.*

> BILL
> God I'm sick of this ACG merger. If
> Johnson doesn't get off my back . . .

As BILL *closes the door to the fridge, he glimpses an appoint-ment card from Beth's gynecologist pinned on the door.*

> BILL
> I'll . . . I don't know, it's a madhouse
> down there . . . That's right, you had
> the doctor's appointment today.
> What did he say?

BETH *hesitates but continues to work.*

> BETH
> I had to cancel . . . I'm way over my
> head with the Xerox account.

BILL *stands there with drink in hand, staring at Beth.*

> BILL
> I thought it was important.

> BETH
> It was. The account exec is close to
> accepting our designs and . . .

> BILL
> I don't mean your god-damned
> account! I mean the doctor's
> appointment!

>   BETH
> There's no problem here, Bill. I'll
> just make another appointment,
> that's all.

>   BILL
> That's not the point. You knew it
> was important to us. You made the
> thing three weeks ago when we
> decided that it was time . . .

>   BETH
> Wait a minute, there was no deci-
> sion, only that we'd go the next step
> . . . just for information.

>   BILL
> But you said that you wanted . . .

>   BETH
> I said I'm not ready yet! I say it all
> the time but you don't listen to me. I
> said I would think about it. Well, I'm
> still thinking.

>   BILL
> And maybe your day wasn't all that
> busy.

BETH *doesn't answer but continues her preparations.*

>   BILL *(cont.)*
> Beth, this is the right time for us. I
> mean we're both healthy, we both
> make a good living, we have a great
> home for kids. The point is we love
> each other.

>   BETH
> Don't make me feel guilty Bill, don't
> do this. Please don't pressure me.

BILL
This isn't pressure. This is about us
becoming a family.

BETH
I thought we were a family.

BILL *can't answer.* BETH *turns away toward the sink and starts to wash a dish.*

BILL
We're going to settle this now.

BETH *stops her washing but doesn't turn around.*

BETH
I can't Bill. Not right now. Right now
I'm going to wash this dish. If you
want to help me, you're welcome to
but I am going to wash this dish and
that's all.

BILL *doesn't reply.* BETH *turns, plate in hand, and slowly reaches over as if to hand it to him.* BILL *just stares at her, lost in thought. Slowly the plate slides from her hand to the floor and she walks out of the kitchen.*

FADE TO BLACK

Let's start with the basic assumption that you've read this two-and-a-half page scene cover to cover. The first time through, you read for basic understanding, continuity, and pace. You put the pages down and you ask yourself, "What is this scene about?" You have a basic scene: Man/woman—husband/wife—discussing whether or not to have children. No choices have been made; all that's done is to reiterate what is in the script: husband and wife's discussion about children. He wants them now, she feels pressured. This has nothing to do with choice. This is a given, what is written on the page. Simple facts.

The trap that some actors will fall into during film and especially television auditions is that they will magnetically be drawn toward the obvious generic choice—meaning your everyday husband who wants a child or your career-oriented woman who wants to work. Actors tend to be a bit insecure until they get a handle on the scene. That tendency leads them to play themselves as the character (personal truth) wanting or not wanting generic children. Why play character truth when you can more easily play personal truth? Because playing the easy choice is not necessarily the best choice. The objective is to get away from playing the clichéd, obvious choices and to look more specifically at all the possibilities available. Only then will you make specific choices. Let's examine the first choice you need to make.

1. Character Choice

The first choice is *character choice*. And it's the first choice because you can't make any other choices until you've made this one. How can you possibly know what your character wants until you know who your character is? It is also the most important choice because it is the character's behavior that will eventually tell the story, and it is the character that the director is looking for in the audition process.

Let's take a look at Bill in our scene. Who is he? Character choice seems as simple as that. Who is he? But it's not enough to answer he's an athletic, good looking, forty-five-year-old, yuppie lawyer. That's not a choice. That's a rehash of the character description written in the script. It's still not specific enough, it's still generic. How many forty-five-year-old yuppie lawyers do you think there are? Millions!

The more specific you get with your choices, the more interesting and unique your final performance will be. Certainly when you're looking at auditioning for a film or television role, "interesting and unique" goes a long way in capturing the producer's and director's imagination and attention. They will have anywhere from five to fifty actors reading for this character and the person who comes in with interesting and unique choices is the person who is going to get the role.

In determining your choice, it is first necessary to break character down into two parts: the external and the internal.

EXTERNAL

The external component of character choice is anything that cannot be motivated internally. In other words, something that is layered externally on the character without his control; for example, a limp or unusual gait (Daniel Day-Lewis in *My Left Foot*), a physical deformity (*The Elephant Man*), a way of moving that's integral to the character's physical form (Anthony Hopkins' stiff, formal butler in *The Remains of the Day*). Similarly, any kind of speech pattern, regionalism, or accent (Meryl Streep in *Out of Africa* or *The Bridges of Madison County*) is an external part of the character's makeup and, as such, exists as an unmotivated, integral element of the character. Laura's limp in *The Glass Menagerie* is part of the way she walks, not motivated by pain, and her Southern accent has been part of the way she talks since she learned her speech patterns as a young child. These are external character choices that are not controlled by an internal impetus.

I remember stories about how Henry Winkler first got the part of Fonzie in "Happy Days." He had done the movie, *The Lords of Flatbush* and felt Fonzie was similar to his character in the film (street character, leather jacket, greased hair, etc.). He wanted to audition for the part, but the producers didn't see Henry as the Fonz; they wanted a Sylvester Stallone type (also in *The Lords of Flatbush*). As the story goes, his agent kept trying and trying to get Henry an audition. When finally the producers, as a favor, let him audition, Henry came in having worked up a unique, external way of movement for the character (that worked with his internal choices as well). He felt that Fonzie would lead from the hips or more accurately, from the groin. And so after a short chat, the producers, who had no intention of giving Henry the part, asked him to read. Henry turned away for a moment and when he turned, before he even said a word, with just his physical posture, he had the part. The story points out the importance of a creative use of an external character choice.

With Bill and Beth in our sample scene however, the opposite situation could also apply. It may very well be the case that the scene actually calls for characters who are not far removed from the "average" thirty- to forty-year-old yuppie couple. In this instance, making a very strong, unique external character choice may not be appropriate. The producers may want fairly traditional external choices with interesting twists for the internal characteristics.

INTERNAL

Many acting theories will tell you that the character's externals are of great help in unlocking the internals of the character. This might include the character's clothing, the way he wears his hair, makeup, or the way he walks and talks. If you're playing William F. Buckley, Jack Kennedy, Amelia Earhart, Princess Diana, or Steve Erkel, once you get the character's vocal patterns set, you can use that as a way of helping you slip into the internal parts of the character. Just remember, there is a great difference between an impersonation and the real behavior of a character.

As my definition of acting is *to be*, it's clear I believe in the concept proceeding from the internal to the external. So I build the character from the inside out. Even though external character choices are an important component, the internal characteristics are what ultimately form the character, as these personality or character traits will eventually translate into the character's behavior. The more you know about your character, the more specific he is to you, the more real you will play him, the more believable he will be, and the more you'll be able to behave like him.

If you happen to have a major role in a feature film and have three months for preparation, you can do a great amount of research. If you're playing Jack Kennedy or Amelia Earhart, you can read books, view vast numbers of videos and films and learn everything available about them. If you're playing a fictional character, such as a wizened old detective or a tough street prostitute, you can research the lives of living people and, through interviews and observance, gain vast amounts of insight into your character.

But if you're in a cold reading with twenty minutes to prepare an audition, you have to have a method of preparing a character and making the proper character choices that is a lot more practical and efficient.

The first thing you have to decide is *how am I different from this person*? Go back to personal truth versus character truth. If the character in the scene behaves exactly like you would, given that set of circumstances, if you could use the old Stanislavsky "If"—"If I were that guy, and married to that girl, (or vice - versa) how would I behave?" If you can say, "I would think and feel exactly the way he or she does; that is, their behavior would be the same as mine," then you can use personal truth. If the answer is, "a little" or "somewhat" or "no," then you must use character truth. Over the twenty-plus years as a working actor in Los Angeles, playing roles from one line bit parts (Reporter #1) to a regular character on a TV series, I could have used personal truth most of the time. But the question that always comes to my mind is "How interesting am I?" Just because you would behave the same way the character does, maybe you would want to play a character who has a different personality from yours. As long as it works within the givens of the script, it might be more interesting for the part and for you, the actor, as well.

There is an acting guru in Los Angeles whose total acting theory revolves around the supposition that there is no character, there is only you and who you are as the character. His goal is to teach his students how to put themselves on the screen. Some of what he says is very useful, but it is also limiting. As actors, we bring as much of our own nature and experience as we can to the creation of our characters. But when faced with a character that possesses personality or character traits that are not part of our own makeup, we must create those missing traits. If you are going to play a psychotic killer, you have a lot of work to do.

This is where talent, creativity, and intelligence come into play. It's your choice who you play. If you play yourself and your choice works for the scene, if the producers and director like it—then you'll get the part. But even if you are a forty-five-year-old yuppie like our character Bill, you still might want to make a more interesting choice as to who Bill really is. There is a great range of possible personality traits you could give Bill or Beth, and the scene would change accordingly, sometimes subtly and sometimes quite dramatically. A friend of mine once said that given the absence of time in these situations, he looks at the differences rather than looking at the similarities between himself and the character. What is different, he programs into his computer; what is similar, he trusts will remain.

I've adapted a shorthand method for working on character choice that can be used in both the limited time before an audition and then expanded for use when you have more time available once the role is yours.

POSITIVES - NEUTRALS - NEGATIVES

I call this approach the *positives, neutrals*, and *negatives* of the character. The positives are traits that are socially accepted—traits which we would like to find in ourselves and others and traits that motivate the character to success, happiness, and fulfillment. Conversely, negative traits are those that take away from or diminish the character's capacity to thrive. And the neutrals are character traits that can sometimes be positive and sometimes negative.

I first look at everything that's written by the screenwriter about the character: I look at everything the character says and does, everything that people say about him, and I glean as much information as I can from the text. For your own development, I suggest that you practice this method on paper first; when you become adept you will be able to make the list mentally under the pressure of an audition. Go down to the library or the local university and check out a screenplay that you don't know at all so you won't have preconceived ideas about the characters. Copy it, take it home, and write all over it. The more you work with a screenplay, the more you will be able to see through the maze.

Next, start to fill in the blanks. What are the positive character traits, the positive personality traits? In consideration of time, you may want to concentrate on those traits that actually define the character. Most of us could attribute almost any descriptive adjective to ourselves. We've all been arrogant, loving, egotistical, warm, destructive, and quiet at some time in our lives. But would we define ourselves in these terms? One of the first exercises I use in my classes on character is for each actor to define himself with the following technique: free-associate and write down as many character traits as you can that come to mind. Then pick the top ten or fifteen choices that most closely describe you. The results are often revealing and sometimes edifying. You tend to learn a lot about yourself in the process. Be honest and probe. After you've finished, ask yourself, "Is that really me?" Once you can define yourself with this technique, you will be able to define your character in the script more easily.

Here are some positive traits you could conceivably attribute to Bill. They are by no means the only ones, nor are they necessarily the *correct* ones. That is the point of this book: they are only one set of choices for this particular moment. They could, and probably would, change as exploration continues into the character's behavior.

Positives
Intelligence - Analytical
Successful
Good sense of humor
Sensitive
Caring
Loving
Athletic
Romantic
Moral
Articulate

Obviously all positive traits make Bill a boring, one-dimensional character. You want to develop and play three-dimensional characters. What if Ben Kingsley had played *Gandhi* as a perfect being, another Jesus Christ? We wouldn't have had the three-dimensional, real human being that was Gandhi.

The opposite of the positive traits are the negative. For example, along with all Bill's positive traits, he also might be impatient, which leads him to anger quickly. You may not choose to call it a bad temper, only that his impatience tends to lead him to eruptions of temper. Here's a list of possible negative traits that you might choose for Bill:

Negatives
Impatient
Arrogant
Condescending
Chauvinistic
Reactive
Procrastinating
Willful

Now we come to the interesting part. I think neutral traits are fascinating because they are the contradiction that creates the real shading of character. As an example, I might attribute "competitive" to Bill. I think a competitive spirit is a tremendous asset to have on your side, but with a lack of control, competitiveness can also be an irritating characteristic that definitely becomes a negative. Neutrals thus become the nuance that adds immeasurably to the character and therefore to the scene.

Neutrals
Ego
Outspoken
Competitive
Traditional
Willful

Looking at Bill's ego, we can establish that he's got a strong ego and is a confident person. If you take that to an extreme, then he's egotistical or self-centered, which is a negative. The positive side would be confidence; the negative would be egoism. So maybe he's in the middle, meaning he does have a strong ego, but it sometimes gets out of proportion or out of control. The same may be true of the terms "outspoken" or "direct." If you said he was an honest, straightforward person, always saying what he means, it's a positive; but if you took that to a negative extreme it could be tactless or insensitive.

This is *one* version of Bill. Now create your own list for Bill and Beth.

Bill			**Beth**		
Positive	Neutral	Negative	Positive	Neutral	Negative

Just by thinking about the positives, neutrals, and negatives you will develop in your own mind a three-dimensional person who is specific and concrete. Obviously you have done something like this exercise many times for roles you've played on the stage. Just keep in mind we're constantly working with a time restraint in auditions as well as on the set. And the more quickly and clearly you understand the character, the more easily you will be able to internalize your choices and behave as that character.

This technique works very well even for the smallest of parts. I remember reading for Reporter #1 on an episode of "St. Elsewhere." All reporters are not the same, but with only a few lines, finding something unique about this person was a test. I decided to choose strong negatives to add a little bite to the character (willful, aggressive, insensitive, combative, egotistical, and rude). I was taking a chance because smaller parts tend to be written as exposition characters who fade into the woodwork and are not focused on. Well, it worked out, and the character was unique and provocative. I got the part and eventually did four more episodes based on the work I did on the first part. The point is choices enable you to stand out in the audition from the other fifteen people who will read for the part. But any choice is a gamble. If you play safe, you can lose to another actor who made a more interesting choice. You can make a unique and creative choice and possibly lose out to a conformist. Or you never had a chance anyway because your hair was too dark! There's no such thing as fair and there's no sure thing in this business.

Once you have decided upon the positives/neutrals/negatives and feel secure about who this character is externally and internally, you can go on to the other choices. Just remember, character choice is the primary one to be made—*all other choices follow from it.* It is also the one choice that most influences the decision of the producers and director as to whether or not you will be cast. They are looking for the character, whoever he or she is. If your other choices are slightly off or inaccurate, they can ask for adjustments. Their main focus is that character—and that's why character choice comes first.

2. Character Relationship

Now that you know who your character is you can ask the questions: Who are the other people in the scene? What is their relationship to my character? What does my character think and feel about them? This is character relationship. Here again, many actors tend to fall into the trap of obvious, nonspecific, clichéd choices. Your character-relationship choice for Bill should not be limited to "Beth is Bill's thirty-seven-year-old wife for ten years." Again, these are just the facts about their relationship. They are not specific enough. To bring more specificity and depth to their relationship, you need to decide what Bill thinks and feels about Beth. In making these decisions, two elements—the past and the present—need to be thought out.

PAST RELATIONSHIP

It is extremely important to differentiate between the past and the present in character relationship. It's the old assumption problem again. Actors are insecure by nature and tend to rush their choices. If they see an argument in the scene, they sometimes make the leap that the characters don't like each other. The past relationship deals with how the characters thought and felt about each other yesterday, last week, last month, last year—*before* the scene begins.

One could make a plausible choice that in the past they always argued about everything; that was the way their relationship worked. Because he's quick to anger and she understands this, they will have these long drawn-out arguments every time they have a discussion.

One could also make the choice that they never argue, that these are people who discuss everything and never argue, that this is the first argument they've ever had and it is atypical to their relationship. Both choices are interesting, both are valid, and both will create quite different dynamics in the scene.

This is why it's very important to understand the past relationship fully: What is their relationship before the scene even starts? What was it like this morning? What was it like yesterday—or last week? Or the last time they talked about children? Are they very close? Have they always been? Do they tell each other secrets? Are they very intimate with one another, not just sexually but in the way they communicate? Are they secure with one another in their relationship? Have the years been good, and are they growing together or are they drawing apart? It is particularly important to select these choices before you make the choice of what their present relationship will be during the scene because the past affects the present.

Many people make mistakes in character relationship choices that fundamentally alter the screenwriter's intentions of the scene—especially in the type of scene that I am using as an example. Again, there is an assumption on the part of many actors and actresses that just because characters like Bill and Beth have an argument in the audition piece, Bill and Beth are having marital problems. That can be a very wrong choice to make in the scene. Characters that are negative toward one another run the risk of alienating the audience. Clearly the writer expects you to find and play his choice but it is not always apparent. A lot of the background character relationship is yours to manufacture. In that case, bite the bullet and make a choice. Remember, clichés abound where there is no choice.

PRESENT RELATIONSHIP

The other element of character relationship is the present relationship. Obviously, there is more information in the text about the present relationship because of the inherent behavior of the characters as written. But it is important not to anticipate at the beginning of the scene what eventually transpires in the middle or end. Clearly Bill and Beth's present relationship changes as the scene progresses. But the question is, what does he think and feel about her during the time frame of the scene? What does she think and feel about him? In other words, he could be very frustrated, and angry with her, resentful and a bit rejected by the time he realizes she purposely missed her doctor's appointment. And she could be defensive and resentful at him for pushing her into a decision. But any negative emotions felt in the heat of the moment could have nothing to do with their basic feelings about each other.

Again, you can't make that choice until you define who your character is. How does your character react to this kind of pressure and this kind of an argument? If you're playing Bill and you've made a choice that he's very stable, reserved, talks things out, has no temper, and is analytical about discussing conflicts, then the scene will be fundamentally different from the previous choice—that he's aggressive, domineering, arrogant, and always gets his way. Character relationship is often overlooked in most acting theories, but it is close to character in its importance to the playing of a scene correctly.

3. Objective

Once you know who your character is and what his relationship to the other characters in the scene is, the natural progression is to choose your objective. What does he want? A number of acting methods consider objective (or intentions) as their primary element. Robert Lewis, the great teacher, director, actor, and member of the august Group Theatre, gives it so much emphasis that he clearly states in his acting textbook, *Advice to the Players*, "While it is true that feeling is an ingredient of performing and it is certainly true that you will often arrive at your intention through character work, I put the most emphasis on intention. . . . It is, in fact, your reason for being on the stage. . . . The sense of the play is carried forward through the intention, no matter how much emotional content is there to give it body. A wrong intention, or the inability to act with intention, can distort an entire scene or a whole play." Lewis went on to describe intentions. "Some call this element of the craft 'objective.' Others refer to it as the 'action' (inner action, they mean, not physical action). Still others simply say it's the subtext."

It is important if you are used to the concept of intentions that you understand the difference between intentions and the use of objectives as I use them in film technique. Lewis's intentions are thought declarations of what the character wants. And that's fine for theatre but it is not specific enough for film and television. If a character says, "Let's get married," the actor can't be thinking, "I want Debbie to know that I love her enough to marry her." That's not how most people think; it's a statement of intent more than a thought pattern. Remember, the only thing you should be doing is thinking and feeling as the character. You need to be specific because a director might want to film a section of the scene that is only a very small part of a beat of a scene—maybe two lines, or one, maybe just a look, maybe just a small thought transition. With separate objective and subtext choices, it doesn't matter what he wants to cover, or from where. You know what your character's behavior is from moment to moment.

For our discussion, we're defining objective as *what the character wants, needs or desires*. Objectives usually relate to the other person in the scene but sometimes not. If the inherent dramatic conflict in the scene is based on the characters versus their environment, or versus other characters who are not in the scene at the time, then your objective has to do with solving conflicts that don't relate to the character relationship of the person with you in the scene. If the conflict in our Bill and Beth scene was based on the problem of infertility rather than a disagreement between them about whether to have children, the objectives would relate to Bill and Beth dealing with how to get pregnant. They wouldn't necessarily have a problem with each other, but with the confusion and frustration of medical science.

There are three basic objectives to work with: the super objective, the overall objective, and the action objectives. The first deals with the entire screenplay, so does not affect an individual scene that may be found in an audition situation. The second and third are more specific to the scene and need to be defined.

SUPER OBJECTIVE

Each character has a *super objective*. The super objective is what the character wants, needs, or desires *in terms of the length and time of the play*.

In our situation, we don't know what is happening in the context of the entire screenplay. Bill's super objective could be a more stable family life, or if he senses his marriage is in trouble, a renewal of love and intimacy in his marriage. You could choose many possibilities for both Bill and Beth. But as an exercise, let's look at a classic play like *Romeo and Juliet* and make a choice. There are many interpretations of what Romeo's super objective might be. For the sake of discussion, let's say that his super objective is "to discover and find meaning to his life" or "To find his place in life." Romeo wants to discover what's outside his friends, family, and city. He knows there is something else, and he wants, needs, and desires it. His super objective can turn into his overwhelming love for Juliet, but if you look at it in the broader context, Juliet is the result of his discovery.

OVERALL OBJECTIVE

The next objective is the *overall objective* of each individual scene, that is, what the character wants at the moment in time that constitutes the scene. The actor does not play an overall because an overall is an overview of the character's objective, used to clarify the actor's understanding of the scene. It can be expressed simply and clearly in a declarative description, usually related to the super objective of the character. In our scene, Bill's overall objective might be "to get Beth to agree to have children."

ACTION OBJECTIVES

Our third objective is more specific still and becomes the main driving force for the character's behavior. Unlike super and overall objectives, *action objectives* are played by the actor moment to moment. Individual action objectives are *what the character wants, needs, and desires, moment to moment, expressed in an action verb.*

Your first individual action objective is your *opening objective.* The reason I'm this specific is that it is important to begin the scene properly. One of the major problems that actors have is anticipating the middle of the scene at the beginning. Actors start to look at major conflicts and arguments, and the tone of those conflicts starts to creep in too early. Anticipation can ruin a scene. (*Telegraphing* is another term often used.)

So start the scene correctly by looking at the opening objective. As Bill walks through the door and leafs through the mail, what is his opening objective? It may have nothing to with the overall objective. Many writers want to establish a natural sense of how their characters behave and relate to one another in the normal give and take of everyday life. Once that is established, they interject the inherent dramatic conflict.

That is exactly the case in this scene. We could assume the only thing Bill wants is a cold drink and a shower, and Beth needs to get the dinner on the table because she's late. Neither one of them know that they're going to get into an argument about children.

In many cases, however, individual action objectives do relate to the overall objective; the moment-to-moment objectives try to accomplish the overall objective.

Let's look at action objectives. They are called action objectives because they are expressed by an action verb: *To - Action Verb*. To convince, to hurt, to demand, to love, to seduce, to rejoice. I've given you a long but partial list at the end of the book. (See Appendix A.) Try them out and add to them. A verb that may seem active and interesting to me may seem ineffective to you. The point is, we've been talking about making active, interesting choices, and this is the place. As objectives are the engine that drive the scene forward, active objectives are essential. One of the toughest acting problems to solve is tempo, rhythm, and pacing. Some actors have a terrible sense of timing to a scene—they just don't have a feel for it. Objectives can solve many of those problems. If you've got a good active objective working for you, the scene will move inextricably forward. Remember also that with matching problems, consistent use of objectives will help you be consistent in each take, angle after angle.

By comparison, let's look at "passive" verbs (passive meaning no action) with possible active verb alternatives.

Passive verbs	**Active verbs**
to say	to convince, manipulate, argue, confront
to give	to help, reward, present
to be kind	to care, bolster, comfort
to tell	to admit, alibi, rationalize
to offer	to bribe, manipulate, assist

You can see by this short list that *to tell* and *to say* don't motivate the character to action. Any objectives that start with *to be* (to be kind, to be angry, to be nice, to be happy) imply a state of being and are inherently passive because, as an actor, you can't play a concept or an idea, you can only play an action (verb). To convince, to force, to manipulate, to urge, to love, to reject, to excite—these are the kind of objectives we can play that will help create a "through line of action" in the scene.

Back to our scene. As Bill comes in the door, what does he want, need, or desire at that very moment? If the issue of children hasn't even crossed his mind, he might very well want to relax, to unwind, to forget the day's problems, or to drink. But if you play the whole scene with passive verbs (to get a drink, to read the paper, to go to sleep) there will be no inherent dramatic conflict. Characters who don't want anything are window dressing. It's the transition out of passive objective choices into active ones that lay the foundation to inherent dramatic conflict.

Bill and Beth begin their little discussion about what the day was like, and all of a sudden, subtextually, Bill thinks, "That's right—she went to the gynecologist and we can get started on making our baby." So, he makes a transition—an objective transition: He no longer wants to relax and have a drink, he wants to discover or to plan or to understand. He says, "That's right, you had the doctor's appointment today. What did he say?" You can't say his objective is to have children, that's not specific enough. What does he want at that exact moment?

Most acting theories will tell you that the definition of a "beat" of a scene relates directly to what the character wants, his objective. You could look at our scene and see that there are clear demarcations between the beats. The first ends on Bill's line about the doctor's appointment, the second ends with Beth saying, " I'm not ready yet," and the third goes to the end. Here, the first beat gets us into the scene and establishes the characters and their relationship, while the second and third center on the conflict and its effect on the characters. All of the action objectives tend to relate to accomplishing the overall objective. The actor must then make those objectives "important" to the character, thereby driving the scene.

RISKS AND STAKES

Any time you talk about objectives you need to include the elements of *risks and stakes*. How important is it for the character to accomplish his or her objective? In our scene, if Bill wants to convince his wife to have children, how important is it to him? What risks and stakes are involved? Is this a situation where he's so desperate to have children that if she doesn't agree it could be reason for divorce? Or is it that Bill would like to have children, but his relationship with Beth is more important? Yes, he wants to convince her, but if he can't, that's the way it is; maybe another time. As you can see, we would have two different scenes because the motivation driving the character would be quite different.

Beth's risks and stakes are equally important here. If she's more interested in her career right now but still would like children in the near future, the risks and stakes wouldn't be elevated. But if she is afraid to have children, or secretly doesn't want them at all, the stakes would increase considerably.

Clearly the use of objectives is relevant in theatre work. Many of the concepts and theories I'm talking about here are not mutually exclusive to film and television. However, there's a greater need to be more specific in film. Objectives keep the motivation for behavior specific and consistent over the course of an extended shooting schedule.

Up to this point we have examined:

Character: external and internal; positives, neutrals and negatives
Character relationship: past and present
Objectives: super, overall for each individual scene, and individual action objectives

If you're clear who your character is, what his relationship is to the other people in the scene, and what he wants, you're 90 percent there. These are the major choices that an actor must make to define any given scene. The final three choices deal with translating those choices into consistent, repeatable behavior.

4. Opening Emotion

The fourth choice for the actor involves the *opening emotion* to the scene. As the opening objective must be very specific and clear in your mind in order to get the scene going in the proper direction, so must the opening emotion be very clear for the same reason. What, specifically, is the character feeling as he enters to begin the scene? For example, you can choose from a whole list of emotions Bill is feeling at the start of the scene: tired, frustrated, weary, resentful (of his boss), stressed, worried, bewildered, harassed, edgy, relieved, discouraged, or others depending on who Bill is and what happened to him today.

In film and television we often have scenes that don't start when the characters meet. Most scenes are already in progress. The characters are talking, loving, or discussing and the writer will cut in the middle of their discourse or, especially in soaps, even in the middle of an argument. This is why it's very important that you start the scene correctly and why I give strong emphasis to the opening emotion: you don't want to anticipate emotionally by playing what's happening in the middle of the scene at the beginning of the scene. We're trying to stop anticipation and play moment to moment. In order to begin the scene correctly you start from a basis of emotional truth.

5. Transitions

The fifth choice is *transitions*. In any well-crafted scene, the writer will use transitions to create rhythm and tempo. As we know, any scene played with one action, one objective, or one level of emotion tends to be boring. Sometimes, in film, we see cutaway scenes that are too short for any transitions, but in the main, a developed dialogue scene has at least one major transition. And it's the transitions—the peaks, valleys, and resulting through line —that build a scene's momentum and therefore its interest. Transitions are changes and it is the changes in the plot, in the character's behavior, in the character's relationships that allow the story to evolve. In the graph of our scene (see below), the vertical line represents inherent dramatic conflict or tension, and the horizontal line denotes the time frame of the scene. Notice the resulting peaks and valleys. Those shifts are caused by transitions.

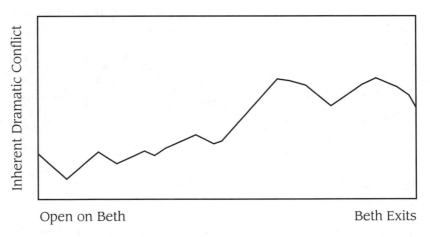

Inherent Dramatic Conflict

Open on Beth   Beth Exits

Now the question is What kind of transitions? I describe three transitions here and they can occur all at the same time, in pairs, or individually.

EMOTIONAL TRANSITIONS

Because the camera registers every nuance of the character's emotional tone and intensity, the emotional transition is of major concern. In the case of our scene, Bill comes home from the office tired and stressed, maybe even a little preoccupied with his work. He's in the kitchen talking to Beth about his job when he sees the doctor's appointment on the refrigerator and an emotional transition occurs. The tiredness and stress are pushed aside by a rush of excitement, anticipation, curiosity, hopefulness, and apprehension. When he senses that Beth missed the appointment on purpose, all the excitement and hopefulness vanish and are replaced with rejection and disappointment. You can play many emotional transition choices in the scene, some obvious and dramatic, some subtle and fleeting. Can you find and/or create them? And once you do, do you have the craft to play them?

OBJECTIVE TRANSITIONS

The second kind of transitions are *objective transitions*. With the third choice we discovered the overall and the opening action objective. Now let's chart the scene for a through line of action objectives. Bill's opening objective was to relax. But once he sees that appointment notice, another objective takes over, and Bill wants to discover. When he discovers that Beth might be resisting having children, there are any number of objectives he could use to accomplish his overall objective. As Beth throws obstacles in his path (to deflect, to retreat) Bill could decide to confront, to punish, to manipulate, to convince, to plead, or to inflict guilt. The objective possibilities are many—which one and when to use them is your choice. If you understand Bill and his relationship to Beth, you'll have some creative and interesting ideas, and they will be part of the reason your interpretation and ultimate performance of the scene will be different from anyone else's.

SUBTEXTUAL TRANSITIONS

The third kind of transitions are *subtextual transitions*. Now we're coming to an element that is much more specific on screen than in the theatre. Think back to the opening discussion on the differences between the two. In a theatre, the audience picks up very little subtext because of the distance from actor to audience. Some changes in the character's thinking process come through the text of the play, but not through the actor's thoughts as so readily happens on film. Remember, because the camera sees into the actor's thoughts and emotions, and the screenwriter takes full advantage of that insight, the actor must have the craft available to make manifest these subtle nuances of thought transitions.

There are major subtextual thought transitions in most scenes—like Bill's subtext as Beth says, "I had to cancel . . ." which might be, "My God, she never intended to go, she never really wanted a baby." But smaller, subtler transitions are often overlooked, and the performance is diminished. Actors miss some transitions because they are misled into thinking that their work is in the words. It isn't: *film and television are subtextual mediums*. And if you are observant and persevere, every once in a while along will come "a moment."

MOMENTS

Sometimes you'll find during one or all of these emotional, subtextual, and objective transitions what I like to call a *moment*. I would define a moment as a unique and interesting instant in time when something electric happens, something very theatrical in the true sense of drama that captures the audience's attention. Although moments usually take place during a transition, not all transitions are moments. Moments are places where the characters are at a crossroads. These places are riveting and have a tremendous effect on the audience. And if you find—if you create—a magical moment, that one moment is enough to get you the job or sometimes an Academy Award. Moments don't come by chance; they are the result of careful, intelligent insight and observation. That insight will dictate your choices, and your choices will create the moment.

In our scene there is a very subtle moment that is hidden and not highlighted by "punctuation," underlining, or the wonderful term that writers love to foist upon actors—(pause). Look at the scene yourself and see what you can find. You may discover something different and possibly more interesting than what's offered here. Look at Bill's speech that starts: "Beth, this is the right time for us. . . ." The possibility of a wonderful subtextual transition with all the earmarks of a moment exists here. But it's subtle, and you can easily run right over it if you're not observant. After Bill has gone through all the logical reasons they should have a baby, he has a subtextual transition. After the line, "we have a great home for kids . . ." he thinks, "Wait a minute, that's not important. What's important is . . ." which motivates his line, "the point is we love each other." If you give that thought the time it deserves and the emotions to reinforce it, the moment will be there.

Moments are certainly what writers and directors are looking for from their actors, and many times an actor will create a moment that the writer never knew was there. But if you miss the transitions that *are* in the script, then the writers will tend to write you off.

I also like to remind actors that *all moments are no moments*. Too many actors try to create moments out of thin air, which leads to over-the-top (overly dramatic) acting. This again interferes with the pacing, the tempo, and the rhythms of a scene. I like to create a scene that has very good pacing and movement—lots of give and take with a fluid, natural pace. Then I find a moment or two, usually around a transition, that will accent the focal point of a scene.

One thing is certain. The director is going to cover any major transition in film and television with a number of camera angles. That means you, as an actor, have to be able to match those transitions and any moments you have created in a master shot, a two-shot, a single, a close-up, an over-the-shoulder, and every other way the director can think up. And, throughout all the shots, your performance must remain consistent, and fresh—as if it were happening for the first time. Knowing where the transitions are clearly gives you a strong indication of where you're going to have to be very specific about matching the physical, subtextual, and emotional levels.

6. Subtext/Speakout

With the completion of the first five choices, you now have an outline of the scene. The first three choices gives the character, character relationship, and objectives. The opening emotion and the transitions begin to translate the first three choices into character behavior. The sixth choice fills in the subtextual through line and gives direction to the entire scene. With subtextual choices, you provide the final element to flesh out the scene. Having already looked at the subtextual transitions, it now becomes a matter of connecting the dots so that there will be a continuous subtextual line. To be more explicit, there are situations that require the use of different terminology to describe two forms of subtext.

SPEAKOUT

To differentiate between subtext when the character *is* speaking (i.e., motivating lines) and subtext when the character *is not* speaking (i.e., when he is listening, when nobody is talking, or when he is alone) I use the term *speakout*, meaning a character's thoughts when he is not speaking.

I borrowed this term from Lee Strasberg and, although I use it differently from him, I think the term is germane and describes this aspect of subtext beautifully. I like the concept that you are "speaking out" what you are thinking, because subtext is a major dynamic of the film and television medium. When directing for stage or a film scene in the classroom, I often ask an actor to verbalize his thoughts when another actor is talking or when no one is speaking, which invariably helps the actor become better focused, sharpen his objectives, and stay involved.

In a cold reading, while the casting director reads with an actor, the director watches the actor to see if he can get a reaction shot from him. He is very interested, even at this audition stage, in seeing how the actor as the character *listens*. He will watch as the camera would, to see what he will eventually have to work with when he gets the actor on the set. If "acting is reacting," then reacting is listening and listening is speakout.

The reaction shot is the editor's best friend. On many occasions a scene has been saved because the editor could cut away from a dull performance to a dramatic and revealing reaction shot. The camera reveals what the character is saying with those Academy Award–winning looks and silences. There is something going on under those silences, and this is speakout. Again, speakout is subtext. They are both thoughts, but by investigating the scene for the different forms of thought, you will better develop the total subtextual level of the character's behavior. By connecting the subtext beneath your lines, with the speakout under your silences, you will create a strong subtextual throughline. During his formative years, Michael Caine was asked by a director, "What are you doing in that scene, Michael?" "Nothing," said Michael, "I haven't got anything to say." "That," said the director, "is a very big mistake. Of course, you have something to say. You've got wonderful things to say, and then *you decide not to say them*. That's what you're doing in that scene."

This is why I stress the three-level system when I talk about the importance of matching takes. There is a behavioral (physical) line that has to match; there's an emotional throughline; and there's a subtextual through line. On stage, with the audience so far away, actors have to learn subtle ways of projection through vocal and physical techniques that communicate their reactions to the audience. Done poorly, actors are open to the criticism of "indicating." Playwrights will even write into the script physical ways in which actors react to what's happening on stage to make sure the audience understands the character's intentions.

In film and television, the screenwriter doesn't need to write any subtextual direction (although some do) because the camera picks up reactions. Ultimately, it is the character's behavior that creates the reaction shot and, as discussed, behavior comes from thoughts and emotions.

Of course, the more preparation time you have, the more you can expand upon the choices and go into depth, clarifying as you work through the scene and the entire screenplay. But you have to make clear choices within these six choices, even if you only have ten or twenty minutes while waiting in an outer office to prepare a scene for an audition. After the part is yours, then you can do the background research; you will have that extra time for more discovery. Remember, though, time is never very plentiful in film and television.

Playing the Choice

When we get to the discussion about final shooting sequences and techniques for shooting a scene on the set, you'll see how these six choices help with the problems of time limitation and matching. They are there if you need to go back to them at any time during the shooting day, even if you've done your master in the morning and can't get to a close-up until the afternoon of the next week. Because you are clear on your choices, you know where you are at every moment in that scene. Your performance will be truthful and believable and your takes will match. It doesn't matter where the director wants to cut in or out of a scene—where he wants to cover with a close-up or what section of the scene he wants to shoot— you will know what you were thinking and feeling and your behavior will be compatible and reproducible.

Some actors who come to the film medium untrained and inexperienced, unaware of film's limitations, may lose out on working again because of inconsistency, matching errors, or trouble with any number of technical problems. Having interviewed many film editors about their relationships to the actor, most agree their jobs are made incredibly easier by actors who are consistent with their takes. They can't believe that working actors don't understand that an editor has to be able to take any piece of film that's shot and cut it into any other piece of film, and that the art of editing demands enormous versatility. Sometimes it is the ability to match takes that makes the difference between a scene being kept in the film, or left on the cutting room floor. Sadly, the loss of an actor's special moment is often due to his own lack of craft.

Now that you've constructed the six choices the question is, How do you play a choice? Many actors are creative and imaginative in making a choice intellectually, but when they come to playing that choice, their craft fails them. That's why the three-level system is so useful. It's very specific. What a character thinks and feels motivates his character's behavior, and all six choices translate into subtextual and emotional work. That's why the six choices are laid out in the order they are. The first three are the reasons why you have to make the last three. First, you have to know who you are, then what you think and feel about the other people in the scene, and then what you want. Finally, you translate that into subtextual and emotional choices.

The only way to play a choice of character, character relationship, or objective is through what the character is thinking and feeling. They are the only tools that an actor has for playing those three choices. How do you play a deranged psychopath? How does a deranged psychopath think and feel? Those two elements alone create his behavior. This is why it is easier to play personal truth than character truth. How *you* think and feel is a lot easier to re-create than creating a new character truth. It is also easier to play character relationship choices that are similar to your own experience as opposed to character relationship choices that you have difficulty relating to. If you are asked to play a man who beats his wife and you aren't married, much less ever had the impulse to strike anyone, you'd have to use character truth rather than personal truth. Look back on our scene. Does Bill relate to Beth as you would to your mate?

By being as specific as possible in using these six choices, keeping good script notes, making intelligent decisions, and creating a full and complete, nonclichéd character, you have a road map of where you are at any given moment. The scene can be shot and matched from any angle, and the director and editor will be delighted. The six choices are where your art becomes involved, where your talent and ability begin to show themselves through your craft. In the end, it comes down to one question: Do you have the craft to make choices and see them on the screen? The answer to that question ultimately defines the actor's ability. And the artistic nature of those choices ultimately defines the actor's talent. If the purpose of art is to illuminate the human condition, then the purpose of the actor is to illuminate that condition through his art. But it has always been through an artist's craft that his art is given expression.

Cold Reading Audition Techniques 5

A n old theatre adage says all you need for theatre is a board and a passion. Unfortunately, for television or film you need considerably more. Because of the cost and technical complexities of production, there are sadly very few chances for screen actors to learn or practice their craft. Most actors coming from the stage want their first screen performance to be the best they can give. But first they have to get the job. That means an audition or as the industry calls it, a *cold reading*.

This book is not meant to be a "How to Get into the Movies" manual. But the cold reading is so essential to the entire process of being a screen actor, it must be discussed. The simple fact is, until you're an established name, you have to audition to work. And auditioning means good cold-reading skills. The problem is that some actors are wonderful once they work on a script and memorize it but lack either the craft or the confidence to be good at cold readings. Even Tony Award–winning Broadway actors complain about not getting film roles because of the dreaded cold reading. Obviously, stage actors have to read to audition for a play too, but the film and television cold reading technique is quite different from what is expected on stage. The truth is, good cold reading skills really have nothing to do with being a great actor. It's just that without that craft, you won't get the job.

What

A cold reading is a casting technique that involves reading from a partial script (one to any number of pages, called *sides*) with anywhere from minutes to days to prepare. The actor reads with a casting director and is viewed by anywhere from one person (the casting director) to many people (director, producers, writers, studio people, and network personnel).

Why

A cold reading is not the best way to audition actors. Good actors with bad cold reading skills fall through the cracks, and bad actors with slick skills sometimes get the part. Feature films tend to have months of preproduction time in which to audition many actors as thoroughly as possible using cold reading, improvisation, long interviews, and screen tests. But TV, because of the lack of time (especially in weekly television series preproduction), must use the cold reading as the most efficient and cost effective means to cast a project.

The normal episodic or sitcom series shoots one episode after another, week after week. But before shooting can begin, a director is given one week of preproduction to prepare a shooting script, make script changes, scout locations, and cast the actors. That translates into one afternoon of auditioning actors. The director will cast an average of ten roles with six actors auditioning for each part—that equals sixty auditions. The cold reading process meets that time criteria.

The Psychology

It's important to understand the basic psychology of the process so that you can adjust your own state of mind and take advantage of any edge available.

Most directors, writers, and producers are basically in awe of what an actor does. They can't do it themselves, and that leads to a certain amazement and respect for the art and its practitioners. This is especially true of film actors because they possess a slightly higher quality of talent and craft than do their television counterparts. But directors and producers are used to TV actors changing lead into gold by taking their mediocre writing and turning it into something better than originally conceived. As a matter of fact, they expect it, which leads to the psychological edge I referred to. An important part of any audition is to retain and reinforce that slight wonderment so they always see you as an artist.

Casting people are saying "no" to the majority of actors they see because there are only so many roles and thousands of actors out there trying to get them. You must realize that you never audition solely for the role you are reading for at the moment. You are auditioning for all the projects all those writers, directors, producers, and casting people will do in the future. So getting the part is not the most important thing, although at the time it may seem that way. Remember, you're in this for the long run, for a career not a job. The attitude you come to the audition with is as important as the choices you make with the reading.

The biggest impediment is fear. As the commercial says, "Never let them see you sweat." If producers and directors smell fear, you've immediately lost that psychological edge. They are businessmen and -women first, and the reality of a thousand dollars per mistake makes them very cautious. Normal adrenaline nervousness or "butterflies" are fine because you can cover for that. What you can't cover up is fear.

It's similar to when you had a big test in college. Remember what you felt when you hadn't read all the material or hadn't studied enough? You walked into the test with zero confidence, sweating bullets, and just praying you were asked the right questions on the test. Now remember what it felt like when you had studied and knew the material cold. You walked in the place with absolute confidence and an attitude that said, "Go ahead, ask me anything . . . I know this stuff!" That's what you've got to feel like when you walk into that audition. It's not about overconfidence or egoism; it's about a nice, easy confidence; you're prepared, you're excited about the choices you've made, and you're looking forward to the reading.

The Process

AGENT

As with the six choices, there is a particular order or structure to the process of a cold reading audition. It begins the moment your agent calls to tell you that you have an audition. Hypothetically, let's assume this is a Tuesday morning and your reading is for 2:00 P.M. the next day. Along with the time and address of the audition, your agent lets you know when you can pick up the *sides* (one or more pages reproduced from the script that make up a scene). In years past, actors received the scripted sides just before they read. These days you can usually get hold of them the day before. In Los Angeles, there is even a new fax service available that sends scenes to the actor's home whenever requested. The capability of getting the script a day ahead is usually the norm, but for the sake of this hypothetical situation, let's say you can't get the script until near the time of the audition.

Your agent will also give you the time and address of the appointment as well as information about the character you're auditioning for. This is valuable information. It is not enough to learn that you're reading a part for a twenty-seven-year-old nurse in an episode of "LA Law." Try to get as much information about that nurse as you can. The agent probably got you the audition because she submitted your picture and resume to the casting director in response to a casting list from the Breakdown Service (a company that gathers all the weekly announcements from the casting directors of the various films and television shows, compiles them into a form that describes the project and its cast of characters being sought, and sends that material to all the agents and managers who subscribe to the service). With the listing of the characters comes a brief description of each character. That's essential information your agent can give you, and that information will dictate how you will dress for the audition.

WARDROBE

I use a statistic that states, you are 80 percent cast, or not cast, when you walk in the door for your reading. Because film is such a visual medium which leads to typecasting, the first impression the producers and director have of you is extremely important. One director told a story about a certain actor who had come into the room and was so perfect for the part that the director said to himself, "Please God, just let her say her name right." Sometimes the reading only confirms the decision to cast you. It's the first gut reaction that sells them. So everything you can do to reinforce that initial impression will help you get cast. The objective is to "slide" or slant what you are wearing towards the character (also makeup and hair for women). If you're reading for that nurse, you don't come in with a nurse's uniform on; you wear something an off-duty nurse might wear. But here we come back to my opening point: What kind of person is this nurse? If your agent has given you a character description from the Breakdown Service describing the nurse as a highly trained and efficient professional who is the tough head of her department, you can make certain assumptions on the physical look you want so that the director will sense, as you walk into the room, that here is a professional, strong, no-nonsense person. Obviously you wouldn't wear a great deal of makeup, or a highly fashioned hairstyle. The right wardrobe, makeup, and hair style are essential to allow people to see you as the character.

TIME

Your agent gives you a time for your audition. That doesn't mean you show up five minutes before your time, grab the script, walk in, and read. You have a lot of preparation to do! How much time is needed differs from actor to actor. Personally, if I can't get the script overnight, I like to have about a half-hour to forty-five minutes to prepare. Much longer than that and I reach a plateau, start to lose my energy, and become dull-witted. Much under a half-hour and I have to rush and can't prepare adequately. How much time you need comes with experience.

SIGN-IN

When you enter the casting office, you sign in (SAG rules), and pick up your sides. Usually there is a secretary or casting assistant at the desk. Be aware—this person could be a valuable information resource. Ask her whether they're ahead of or behind schedule. Sometimes, if the directors are held up on the set, they can be hours behind. The assistant will also be able to tell you who will be reading with you (usually the casting director, sometimes a reader), who will be in the room, how the room is laid out, if a complete script is available, and *most important*, whether he knows anything about the character you're playing. It amazes me how rarely actors take advantage of this resource.

I have found some of these people to be a veritable treasure trove about the project. Some are bright, up-and-coming young casting assistants who sit in on casting meetings, pay attention, and go on to become casting directors and producers themselves. You might get lucky and learn something useful. I learned this one day while waiting to read for a "Dallas" episode. Out of the blue, the secretary said to me, "they're all upset in there because all the actors are reading with too much aggressiveness. They just want a nice guy." After a little friendly follow-up conversation, I finished my preparation and played just what she said, a nice guy. After I read the director said, " Good reading, you're the first actor who didn't try to make something out of the character that wasn't there." I got home and my agent had already called to say I got the part.

PREPARATION

Now that you have the sides of the scene you're to read, what next? One suggestion is to get away from people. Find a place down the hall or outside where you can work in peace and quiet. If you stay around the waiting area, you're only going to get distracted and psyched out.

There is a specific structure to preparing a cold reading which demands a chronological adherence to the order in which you proceed.

1. Read the material, cover to cover. Get the tempo and rhythm—the flow. Read it as you would a novel. Don't start saying your character's lines in your head as you read; forget what your part is and try to get an overall understanding of the scene. Too many actors go directly to their part on the first reading and misunderstand the true nature of the scene, placing undue emphasis on their character's involvement. It becomes the classic tale of not seeing the forest for the trees. Don't hurry this step. Too many mistakes are made later in your choices because you never fully understood the scene in the first place.

2. Now put the script down, settle back, and think, "What is this scene about?" Don't intellectualize here, just give a plain, simple answer to the question: "What is this scene really about?" Remember our discussions earlier about the difference between a play script and a screenplay? Those differences are the reasons why you have to look closely at the entire pages—the dialogue *and* the stage directions. What is

stated by the characters might have nothing to do with what happens in the scene. Maybe the scene is entirely subtextual. Make a choice! Then, read it again! See if you agree with your first instinct. Yes, I have it—the scene is about my husband discovering that I don't want children.

3. Now read the script again, only this time, for the first time, focus on your character in the scene and see if you still think the scene plays the way you thought it would.

4. Now you put the script down and start working on your six choices *in order*:

    1. Character—internal and external
    2. Character Relationship—past and present
    3. Objective—super, overall, and action
    4. Opening Emotion
    5. Transitions—Emotional—Objective—Subtextual
    6. Subtext—Speakout

    You make specific, active choices that essentially will program your computer. You should feel good about going into that reading because you are unique and interesting and because you have made unique and interesting choices. Your reading won't be just like all the others. You must trust that those choices will be there when you need them, that all you have to do is go in there and *be* that character. Just think and feel, and the character's behavior that you chose will come alive.

5. The next step is to verbalize the material and your choices. What sounds wonderful in your head might be awkward when vocalized. Now is the time to verbalize the dialogue and let the emotions and subtext form the phrasing of the lines. You might find that certain vowels are difficult to say when placed next to certain consonants. Get comfortable with the sound of the words, but don't revert to "setting the line" just because you like the sound of it. Stay motivated by subtext and emotions.

6. Figure out whether there is any movement in the scene that will help you. The rule of thumb is to disregard all stage directions. "She moves to him—He lights her cigarette—She kisses him lightly, then slaps him." Don't plan to slap or touch a casting director for any reason. They don't like their space invaded upon and it definitely breaks suspension of disbelief. There will usually be a chair facing the casting director and whoever else is involved with the casting. If you want to sit and do the reading from the chair, the option is yours. Auditions for commercials always use videotape so you have

to be on a mark. Very infrequently casting (West Coast) will use video in film and television readings, so if you want to move around it will be your choice. A lot of movement is not recommended because directors want to see into your eyes as the camera would see. I had a TV series producer tell me that when he auditions actors, he's only interested in the face and eyes because, in television, that makes up most of the shots. On the other hand, if you can stay motivated and believable, movement can add a lot of interest and focus to the reading. The rule is, if movement works, use it. If it makes you uncomfortable or stiff, stay in the chair. Remember that our main objective is to create that suspension of disbelief as much as possible. Anything that takes away from that is harmful.

THE INNER OFFICE

The casting director finally comes out and calls for you. Be there, be ready. Don't make them chase around after you. When you enter the inner sanctum, the casting director will introduce you (assuming your audition isn't a preliminary one in which case you'll be reading with just the casting director in the room). If there are a number of people, don't waste their time shaking everyone's hand; just say hello and sit down.

Remember when I talked about slanting your wardrobe toward the character? The same thing applies to you, or more precisely, your own character traits. Initially, you're an actor first and the character second during an audition. You never know what role they will eventually see for you, but because that first impression is so important and many decisions are made in that moment, slide from your own personality toward the personality of the character you're auditioning for. Don't become the character when you come in the room, but slide toward that character so that they can see the possibility of your playing the character. For example, I was reading for an episode of "Switch" (Robert Wagner, Eddie Albert), auditioning for a feisty, arrogant McEnroe-type tennis player. I couldn't play personal truth because, of course, I don't have that disposition, so I came into that room with just a touch of cockiness and lots of confidence—not too much, don't want to antagonize the casting people. I wanted just enough so that, even before the reading, they were already thinking, "Yeah, this guy could play this character." I guess they believed I could be arrogant and aggressive. I got the part.

Once inside the room, the casting director, producer, or director could ask you a few questions as sort of warm-up or mini-interview. What they're trying to do is see you walk, talk, and chew gum because they know from past experience that who you are is probably what they'll get when they film you on the set. That's another reason for sliding your character to the role you're playing.

If they're not behind schedule, they might ask you something like, "What have you been doing lately?" or "What's happening in your life these days?" or even "What happened to you in the latest earthquake?" It's really not important what they ask, it's only important that you give them some warmth, positiveness, and energy. No fear, no begging. Definitely do not recite your resume as they are very capable of reading. Psychologically, they want to see *you*. I recommend having some interesting anecdote or brief experience ready, just in case. That way, they'll see you talking about something you care about and have some enthusiasm for. Do not apologize for your experience and training (or lack of it). If they ask whether you've starred in any Paul Newman films lately, the answer is *not* no. Never leave them with a negative. If you have the creativity to be an actor, you should be able to come up with a variety of positive answers. I go up against actors all the time who are more experienced or more famous. If anyone thinks I'm going to apologize for my training and experience, they're crazy. I'm proud of what I've accomplished and so should you be. Directors and casting people will sense that too.

THE READING

Finally, they ask, "Any questions? Let's read." If you don't have any questions, no problem—if you do, ask them. Directors love to seem to have all the answers. There can be times when you're not sure of one or a number of your choices, they're not clear in the text and you could play them in a number of different ways. Make the best choices you can, prepare alternative choices, then ask questions and adjust. This does not mean making the director do your work for you. If you ask an obvious or stupid question, they definitely lose confidence in you.

Cold reading is a misnomer—you neither read, nor read cold. It is, instead, a prepared process and a definite skill. An actor with good cold reading skills will only look at the script 20 percent of the time, and when she does it will be "a motivated look." That means that even though the eyes are actually on the script, you don't *drop* your subtext or emotional level. You sustain a through line to the character and her behavior. Although the actor's eyes glance at the script, they don't stare at the script, breaking suspension of disbelief. It's a technique that is easily learned with a little practice. I've taught thousands of actors how to better cold reading skills, and even the worst got better very quickly. It's a motor skill that can be practiced at home as well as in class. Read into a mirror while looking at the page less and less, trying to stay in contact with the mirror as much as possible. You rapidly learn to pick up more and more information with fewer and fewer looks.

Everybody knows you have to look at the script sometimes; casting people don't want or expect it to be memorized; they just don't want your character's behavior interrupted. *Dropping* is a cardinal sin. And there is no need. If you've done your preparation correctly, you know the script. It's not memorized, but with a short deflection of your eyes to the script, you should pick up the next two or three lines. Even in real life we don't continuously stare into another person's eyes for any length of time—we often look away, up, down, or to the sides. Any of those moments can be a motivated look at the script—motivated because you sustain your three levels.

Although, as a general rule, scripts do not have to be memorized, there are a few possible exceptions. I recommend knowing well, if not memorizing, the opening line as well as the closing line. The principle is that after the casting director has seen and talked to you as the actor, you need a transition into the character. Once they say, "Let's read," you can't immediately begin with the first line. Take a moment (don't overdo it), get your character going, think about your opening objective, start your subtext, let the opening emotions flow, glance at your first line, take a beat, and begin. The first time they see you as the character, you want to be focused and complete. You don't want to read that first line. The same applies to the last line. The last impression you want to leave is you as the character, not you as the actor looking at the script, searching for a line.

I also recommend knowing the lines going in and out of any major transitions, especially if they are moments. You don't want to play right up to a great moment, then ruin it by looking at your script.

Eventually, there will come a time when you will be interrupted by either the casting director or director during your reading. The first reaction most actors have is that they've screwed up and everybody in the room thinks they're awful. Wrong! When they interrupt, it is because they see something in you they are definitely interested in and they just want you on the right track. Usually the interruption happens because you made some choice that wasn't what they wanted. They wouldn't stop you if they thought you were bad; they wouldn't waste their time. They want to correct a choice so that the scene works as they see it. They also want to see if you're directable. So if the director says, "Let's stop for a moment here. Beth (the character) is more aggressive, more stubborn . . . she's much more antagonizing to the people around her." No matter whether you thought that's how you already were playing her, you must *adjust* and give them what they want. If you stay the same, they write you off as undirectable, so adjust and feel good about the interruption because you'll know they're interested.

You should also be prepared to "read with a wall." Some casting directors have no background in theatre and don't pretend to; they know they're not actors so they don't try to act. They just "say" the lines—sometimes dully, with no energy and a monotone. It can be unnerving if you aren't expecting it. On the other hand, a number of these casting directors have come from theatre, even acting, backgrounds. During a reading, they can give a nice, evenly-paced reading, letting you dictate the tempo. The important thing, however, is that the director auditioning you isn't paying any attention to the casting director's reading; he's looking at you, even when the other characters in the scene are talking. The director is watching you. Are you listening? Can he get a reaction shot from you? Does he believe you believe? Is there behavior there that he can film? Are you the character?

Finally, the reading is over. Unless you totally bowled them over with your reading and they are applauding madly for your performance, there is an awkward moment when you finish the scene. They usually come up with something noncommittal like, "Very nice, thank you." Now it's up to you to graciously get up, say thank you, and leave the room with as much dignity as possible. It is a very vulnerable moment for most actors because they have just given of themselves, put their talent on the line, and are feeling a little lost without some sort of feedback.

Unfortunately, you very infrequently get much feedback. The producers and director have other actors to read and miles to go before they sleep. They might have loved you or thought you were totally wrong for the part; you may never know. You'll either get the part or you won't. If you do, it doesn't necessarily mean you're a better actor than the others, only that you were the right one for that one part. If you didn't get it, it doesn't mean you were awful. Your physical appearance or your choices could have been wrong for the part. Don't beat yourself up. Whether or not you got the part could have very little to do with your talent. It is out of your control. The important thing is that you showed them good craft and a professional attitude that they will remember down the road.

On the Set 6

Congratulations! You got the part. Now what happens?

In this chapter we will go through the process from the agent's call with the good news, to the end of the first shooting day. As was the case in the cold - reading process, there is a progressive sequence that should be followed in order to take advantage of the little time available to prepare and shoot the scene(s). I must again point out that you can train and practice stage acting almost anywhere at anytime, but screen acting involves a technical environment that greatly diminishes the opportunities for actors to practice and refine their craft. The more you understand and are prepared to face the confusion and chaos that dominates the experience of shooting in a studio or on location, the less those limitations will affect the quality of your work.

Preproduction

AGENT

When your agent calls to tell you that you have the job, he will also explain the financial deal he made with the casting director representing the production company. There can be many elements or combinations of elements that can go into any deal. Obviously there is money, but that depends on whether you're hired on a contract per day, per week, per run of the picture, or a host of other pay schedules. Then there are the credits your agent negotiates such as whether your name is on the credits before the picture or after, starring, co-starring, feature role, and so on. It's a battle that is best left to your agent. In terms of your craft, it's not important what you make, only how you make it.

Your agent also lets you know the number of days and dates you'll be shooting, when the script will get to you, and who will call you to set up a wardrobe fitting. This is all important because it determines the parameters of time you have available for preparation. For purposes of this illustration, we will make the following assumptions: it's Thursday night when you find out you've got the role and you will shoot your two scenes on Monday morning.

PREPARATION

Between Thursday night and Monday morning there are a number of tasks to be performed. Very soon after your agent talks to you, a call will come from the wardrobe people confirming sizes and setting an appointment with you for a wardrobe fitting. This is followed in rapid succession by a complete shooting script sent by messenger to your home. This is important because you have to do some work before that wardrobe fitting.

WARDROBE

I feel it is extremely valuable to do a lot of character preparation *before* I go to the initial wardrobe call because I then have some constructive feedback to discuss with the wardrobe people rather than just my own taste in clothes. The wardrobe people don't mind ideas and suggestions coming out of a character study of what that the character would wear in any given circumstance. They do tend to get particularly touchy about actors who make them chase around trying to accommodate their vanity. They don't want to hear, "Oh I don't look good in that shade of green," or "Can't you recut this suit so I look slimmer?" They don't have the time to deal with an actor's ego.

A friend who was head of wardrobe for a number of television series as well as many feature films always complained about actors who only cared about looking good so that they would eventually become stars. This lady herself had come from regional theatre and felt she could always tell the theatre-trained actors from the Hollywood types—stage actors consider discussion about their costumes to be integral to the process of building a character, while the screen actor worried more about persona. This creative costume designer had to admit that, sadly, with the pace of television, even the most disciplined actor can't fully explore character issues because of the lack of preproduction time.

It is important that you understand that by the time you have your first meeting with wardrobe, they have had numerous production meetings with the director and have a good idea of the character's background, the setting and location, the director's ideas, and the cinemagraphic and lighting concepts that will dictate what color and shade the clothes must be to work well on film. With this information, they have pulled a number of apparel choices from various storehouses and are prepared for your fitting. You, on the other hand, have none of this information, so unless you have a pertinent idea based on solid character study, it is recommended that you accept their decisions graciously.

That is not to say that you shouldn't let your ideas be known. And even if the clothes they chose for you are set, any outfit can be dressed up or down with accessories. Those little touches can say a lot about the character. I once went to a wardrobe fitting for "Wonder Woman" where I was to play a "bad guy." The wardrobe people had chosen a gray charcoal suit, white shirt, and black tie for my character. Their selection didn't exactly fit my character choices because, physically, I am not your typical-looking thug. I tend to lean toward the white bread, clean-cut, All-American WASP type. I can play the internals of a "bad guy," but the externals are not a good fit . . . remember why there is typecasting. Further complicating the issue was a rather tough, mean looking character actor they had cast to play my partner in crime. They were going to dress him in a similar fashion, so I was anticipating a rather comical-looking duo, dressed like twins, with yours truly looking like a college boy dressed up as a Halloween mobster. Granted, the style of "Wonder Woman" was certainly cartoonish, but I still didn't think the initial wardrobe choices would work. Since I had read the entire script over a few times, my character choices were that this guy was a drifter and loser with little education and background who had gotten by over the years with personality, physical intimidation, and an amoral conscience. When he finally talked his way into a good-paying job, albeit nefarious, he would spend his money on clothes and jewelry to reinforce his ego. I mentioned my version to the wardrobe person with specific evidence and character descriptions at the ready. He thought my reasoning sound and together we rummaged through many styles of suits until we found something that fit the character. The result, of course, is TV history! I still am amazed that I didn't win the Emmy that year.

SCRIPT STUDY

When the script arrives at your door, you can begin the major task of script preparation. When you prepared for the cold reading, you had a problem of time and lack of information as only a few pages of script were available. You basically were making educated guesses with the choices you made. Now you have the complete script and more time to work with it. You need to take advantage of that invaluable time.

The same process applies at this stage as it did during the cold reading. The first thing you have to do is read the entire script *cover to cover.* Read for absorption, understanding, and continuity, and do not focus on your character's scenes. Don't analyze anything as you read. Read it, uninterrupted if possible, as you would a novel for overall comprehension. This is a very important step that can't be overstated. This reading should give a good understanding of the style, the pace, and the character's true nature. What was only hinted at in the few scenes you saw at the audition, you now can confirm with the entire script.

Read it again and this time focus on how your character's scenes relate to the storyline. There is a significant difference between a major character that is followed throughout the story and is directly affected by the inherent dramatic conflict and a minor character that appears in a few scenes, has no impact on the other characters or the action, and exists only to sustain a certain scenic reality (cops, reporters, secretaries, family members, co-workers, etc.). They are important to the logic of the script, but do not affect the major characters or the outcome of the plot. It's important to know this because of the focus that is expected of your character. You, of course, play him with no less truthfulness or believability, but you make choices as to character, character relationship, and objectives in proportion to the focus intended. Clearly you wouldn't play a waiter whose action was to interrupt a dramatic moment between Robert Redford's and Glenn Close's characters at a restaurant with any more uniqueness than it would take to motivate a real waiter to say,

"Will there be anything else?" In a scenario like this, the waiter should blend in with the furniture. The director will probably never show the waiter completely, just an indication of a waiter with the camera remaining on the central characters where the real drama is centered.

With the understanding of your character and his scenes in the context of the entire story, it's time to do your choice work. Now, however, you have a much clearer perspective for those choices. For one thing, you already auditioned for the part and got it. That should tell you the choices you made for the cold reading are probably a good guide to follow, which is not to say there shouldn't be further exploration. Also any choice work done should be made with the awareness that any choice is a *tentative* choice. Because everything can and often does change on the set, you can't set your choices in stone. Definitely do the work and make the choices, but be ready, willing, and able to adjust those choices when required.

Break each scene down, starting with the first choice— character—and finishing with subtext. Start with the choices you had at the audition and build upon them with additional information gathered from the script. With character, you can go much farther with your delineation. What do the stage directions say about your character in other parts of the script you didn't see before? What do other characters say about your character? What is your character's behavior in any scene you hadn't seen before? Anything helps that adds and fills out the holes of your character. I usually sit down and write out a character description, even for the smaller parts. The exercise is good because it keeps you away from playing clichés and forces you to develop three-dimensional characters.

MEMORIZATION

The next and probably the most important step is to memorize your lines. I cannot stress strongly enough how necessary this step is. The whole three-level system depends on total, confident memorization. It is impossible to be thinking the character's thoughts and feeling the character's emotions while trying to remember your lines. It just doesn't work, and the result is always disastrous. There is nothing so terrifying as being on a movie set with hundreds of people scurrying around intent on one goal—to film a scene—and here you are, making mistake after mistake, all because you don't know your lines well enough. It can ruin your day and put a real damper on your career, especially with that director, casting director, and producer. Remember, "Show up on time, *know your lines,* and don't bump into the furniture." It's your job!

I have always had a problem with memorization. (I think I was hit on the head too many times playing hockey as a youth.) My short-term memory is sluggish and I just don't pick up lines very quickly. It's not a problem as long as I take enough time and get those lines down cold. One of the tricks I use to memorize is to read the scene (all the characters' lines) into a tape recorder a couple of times (without any particular phrasing). Then I just listen while I'm at home or driving in my car. After I have the overall flow of the scene, I rerecord the scene with just the other character's lines. This way, I can listen, as my character would (speakout), and respond naturally. I'm not listening for "cues," I'm listening as my character would which motivates the reason for my next line. That way, my lines become an extension of the overall scene and there is a natural throughline of direction. I can also practice my six choices and adjust anything that is awkward, forced, or not believable. Remember the concept of developing your own critical eye and being self-directed. It begins to pay off here.

As strange as it sounds, there is a complete acting technique based on this very exercise. Jeremy Whelan in his book *Instant Acting* writes, "You read your lines into a tape recorder, and then you put your script down and act out the scene to the playback of the taped lines. It's emotional surfing."

Now I'm going to say something that may seem to contradict what I've just said. Do not memorize your lines with meaning. What I mean is: do not learn your lines with any particular phrasing, emphasis, or rhythm. If you do, you will be stuck if things change on the set. If you have only the words memorized and then add meaning by the use of subtext and emotions, you can easily adjust to any changes on the set. Because it's so important to have the words just pop out of your mouth without thinking, just as they do in regular conversation, I memorize them so well, I can say them in triple time. Try it with a poem you already know. If you can say it that fast, then you know it so well that you don't have to think about the words. And, of course, that is the foundation of the three-level theory: you think and feel character thoughts and emotions and the character's words and actions will be motivated and believable. Michael Caine says of memorization, "So much of it really is a matter of repetition, of saying the lines over and over again until you're sick of them; until someone can give you a cue, and you say, feel, and react to the whole cycle of events, including those related to everyone else's parts. That confidence is your safeguard against terror."

It's now Sunday night and you've had the "luxury" of three days for preparation and memorization. Now you're only waiting for the assistant director to telephone and let you know your call times. After shooting on Friday night, the production team will usually meet to discuss Monday's shooting schedule. If they will be shooting on location then they have to consider the possibility of switching to an indoor studio set in case of bad weather. That's why they may not call you until Sunday night to give you the final call times.

When the assistant director or some other production person calls, he will usually give you two call times: one for the time to be in the makeup chair and the other for the time your first scene is to be shot. If your call time to report is around 10 A.M. that probably means they (the production team) won't get to your scene until after lunch. However, they want you there ahead of time so that you're completely ready when needed. If your call is 2 P.M. or later, your scene is probably nearer to the end of the day. You're never quite sure as sometimes they might not know exactly when they will be able to squeeze your scene in. The producers paid you for the day, so if they want you sitting in your dressing room all day, in wardrobe and made up, that's their prerogative.

The assistant director will also give you the location and any directions to get there, as well as an emergency phone number. Write everything down and make certain you understand how to get to the location in the morning. With this information, you can work out a time schedule for the next day. I once had a call time for 7 A.M., at a location over two hours away, which meant I had to be up at 4 A.M. and in the car by 4:30 A.M. so I could be there by 6:30 A.M. Do whatever it takes as long as you *show up on time*. There are no excuses; it's part of the job.

Production

Monday morning comes early when you've got a 7 A.M. call and the first scene of the day. You're shooting at Paramount Studios twenty minutes away so it's up to you to be there at least one-half

hour before your call time. I make it a habit to get there even earlier than is necessary because it takes the anxiety out of the experience. I try never to worry about being late; then I have extra
time to look over the set and my preparation again, and I can help
myself to a free breakfast, compliments of the production company. There is usually a crafts service food wagon or food table
available the entire day. Take advantage of it and get there early
enough to sit down and have a little something to eat. I also like
to bring a small carry-bag containing my script, pencil, hairbrush,
and a book to read. There are often hours and hours of waiting
interspersed with frantic moments of shooting.

SECOND AD

The first thing you do when you arrive on location or at the studio soundstage, is to find and sign in with the "Second" (Second
AD or second assistant director). He will be where you will see an
accumulation of people gathering around various production services (dressing rooms, makeup, hair, props, food). Everyone
knows the Second AD; "See that guy in the green shirt over there?
That's Ned, he's the Second." Once you go over to Ned, you introduce yourself and sign in. Make friends with this guy or gal
because he can help you by making life easier while you're waiting to shoot. His job, however, depends on knowing where you
are at all times so, from the moment you signed in, until you're
signed out at the end of the day, you should be in one of three
places: around the staging area, on or around the set, or in
between the two areas. If you're anywhere else, let Ned know.

   Ned is also a great resource of information. The rule of thumb
here is that you ask your questions of the lowest possible person
in the chain of command. The order is Director, First AD, then one
or many Second ADs. Don't ask the director where the toilets are.
On the other hand, you don't ask the Second AD what your objective is either. Ned's job has nothing to do with creativity; he probably will never see anything shot. His job is to keep the flow of
personnel and equipment going so that there is no holdup with
shooting. Ned, however, will be able to tell you where everything
is and, most importantly, whether production is on schedule or
not. One day I showed up on location for a 10 A.M. shoot and the
Second came rushing up to me, "I've been calling your house,
hurry up and get into makeup, you're up next, the lion's sick."
They had planned to shoot two scenes before mine that involved
a lion. When they began shooting in the morning, the lion had a

bellyache and they had to quickly gear up to prepare an alternate scene so they wouldn't lose valuable shooting time. The whole production team's number one job is to provide the people, the machines, and the material to keep that camera rolling.

After Ned tells you where everything is located and any time considerations currently in effect, it is a good idea to find your dressing room. "Dressing room" is the description of any place they can find to give you some privacy. According to SAG rules, it is required you have such a place. Oftentimes it is a little nine-by-twelve trailer or, on location, an even smaller "honey wagon" which means a long semi-truck trailer with six or eight little cubicles built into it. The "stars" get the big motor home rigs. For now, just be content that you have a place to get out of the sun and cool off. Unfortunately, extras sometimes get prodded around like cattle with hardly a place to sit down.

The first thing I do when I get to my dressing room is to check my wardrobe. I didn't do this one day when I was working on an episode of "Paper Chase" and when I was ready to get into my nicely pressed suit, I found out that the pant legs were sewn together. Not my fault, but I still was the one who had to go on the set to block the scene without my pants on. Do yourself a favor and check everything out.

Let's assume here that it's now 6:30 A.M., and everything is on schedule. You don't need to be in makeup until 7 A.M. There is much you can learn in that time that will help you when it's your turn to shoot. Ask Ned who the other actors are in the scene with you. Search them out to see whether they might want to go over the scene. There is an unwritten pecking order here that dictates: if you're higher (according to the size of your role) than another actor in your scene, you ask, "Would you mind going over the scene with me?" If you're lower, you say, "I'm in the next scene with you and I'm available if you want to go over it before we shoot." It's a slight distinction but important nonetheless. As there is usually not enough time to rehearse fully and the director may throw in a lot of changes on the set, many actors don't want to rehearse too much because they are worried about the scene getting dull or mechanical. As I pointed out in an earlier chapter, even a veteran theatre actor like Anthony Hopkins warns about rehearsing too much because it's never the same when you get on the set.

If there is no chance to rehearse, another option is to ask Ned where your scene will be filmed. If the production team is not already shooting on your set, you can get on that set and familiarize yourself with everything. This is especially true if the set is supposed to be your character's home, office, dorm room— anyplace you're supposed to be familiar with. Work with all the props, lay and sit on all the furniture, go in and out of all the doors, and walk around the set getting spatially oriented. Remember, if this is supposed to be your living room, you've been in this room thousands of times and your behavior, while you're in that room, should reflect that. Obviously, if your character has never been to the area before, you may want to stay away from it as long as possible so that you can use that unfamiliarity in your work. Spontaneity is ruined by anticipation. A warning: if you see a set that is taped off and has "hot set" signs on it, don't touch anything because they haven't finished filming on that set and anything moved will cause a problem with continuity.

If all else fails you can always approach the set where they are filming and quietly, unobtrusively observe. But as Michael Caine points out, "Eager hanging-about before you are called is not recommended. Everybody on a film set has a function, and if you don't, you're probably in the way." I think, however, that if you are unobtrusive and can find a spot out of the way, you can learn a lot if it is your first day of shooting. You can see the way the director works, how he handles actors, how fast he expects the actors to work, how his temperament is, and how much input he accepts from the actors. All the answers to these questions will dictate your probable relationship with the director when it's your turn. It's better to know the director hates actors before you film than be surprised with his behavior on the set and have your work affected.

IT'S MAGIC TIME

"Scene 43! Can we have the first team please?"

The First AD calls the actors to the set. The Second AD has given you plenty of warning so you're in makeup, in wardrobe, and now ready to work. This very well could be the first time you meet the director and the other actors in your scene. There will be quick introductions all around and the director will finally say something like, "Well, let's block this out and see what we've got."

BLOCKING

The blocking period can be a fast and furious ride for all con- cerned. Realize that the director is blocking not only the actors but also giving the camera people, lighting people, and sound people their own initial introduction to the scene as well. Most directors, especially in television, work very rapidly because they're trying to direct many people at the same time and want to sustain a flow as they work through the scene. What that means for you is that you have to concentrate absolutely on what he is saying. He will tell you where to move, on what lines, and give you *marks* to hit. A mark is a piece of thin tape which is applied to the floor in front of your feet (usually in the form of a T). Sometimes your mark might be a piece of furniture (sitting in a chair a specific way or your hip touching the side of the couch). There is usually no time to be writing everything down as he positions you throughout the scene. You *must* pick everything up the first time he gives it to you. Try not to be the actor who always asks, "Excuse me for a moment would you? On what line did you say I should move to the couch and sit down?" Directors get very frustrated with actors who don't pick up their blocking quickly and cause them to lose their train of thought. Remember "Don't bump into the furniture"? This is what that part of Spencer Tracy's advice means. You're paid to be able to pick up your blocking quickly and then be able to repeat that action over and over again, hours, days, or even months later.

I listen very carefully to any comments a director makes to the cinematographer as to how they intend to cover the scene with different angles. How much does he intend to use the master shot? Will he cover everything in close-ups or medium shots? If there is a lot of moving around, getting in and out of chairs, how will he cover these moves? And most importantly, what coverage will he use during those few moments or transitions you think are the pivotal points of the scene? If you hear them talking about lots of coverage, especially rises into and out of close-ups, you should be extremely careful to be simple and clean in your physical movements during the master. Everything you do has to be matched and the wilder you are in the master, the more difficult it is to get that physical action to stay within the boundaries of a close-up. Each shot angle has advantages and disadvantages for the actor. Let's look at the four basic camera angles that the actor must deal with most often.

Master Shot ■ The master, sometimes referred to as the establishing shot, is a wide-angle shot that encompasses the action and allows the audience to take in the overview of the scene. There are few restrictions for the actor because the camera is so wide, but, he should be alert for places that the director will cover

Master Shot

with a closer shot. The master also concerns itself with location, characters, time of day, season of year, even temperature. Out of the five senses, film uses only sound and two dimensions of sight—horizontal and vertical. (There is no depth because the screen is a flat surface.) A gifted cinematographer, however, can subtly create the other senses with his art. The actor should be aware of the master's potential and realize that with his character's behavior he can help enhance those sensory details.

Let's say, for example, that during a scene you're walking in the woods. Is your character aware or affected by the temperature? Does he smell anything? What is he tasting? Many times you don't have the chance to work with those elements until you're actually on location and get a feel for the environment. One day I found myself in Yosemite National Park, rappelling down a 200-foot rope, 1,000 feet off the ground, filming a scene for the movie *The Edge*. There was plenty of sensory stimuli to deal with, like vertigo and cold sweat. I didn't have to do a sense memory exercise to be able to feel fear; it came rather quickly when I went over the edge of the cliff. The camera position for the master shot was set up across the valley, a half mile away. And, yes, there

Two-Shot

was coverage. During the close-up, a climbing cameraman was lowered from another rope ten feet away from me for the shot.

Two-Shot ■   On a two-shot (or three-shot) the camera goes in closer and the actors fill up more of the screen. The background is less recognizable in the composition. You will see this shot used quite frequently when there are many characters in one place (around a dinner table, for instance). By shooting a two- or even a three-shot, the director can cover more characters with fewer setups, once again saving time (money).

This is where feature films and television differ. Because of the size of the ultimate viewing screen, film camera angles can widen on all their shots, while television has to stay fairly close for the audience to be able to see into the actor's eyes. As John Ford, the great Western movie director said to one of his cameramen, "I want to see the eyes . . . the eyes tell the story." But in film those eyes can be seen from farther back. With the two-shot the actor has to begin to pay closer attention to physical continuity and matching because the sides of the screen begin to restrict his movements. The frame is getting closer to the actor and on camera, the distance between two people engaged in a normal conversation needs to be a lot closer than would be comfortable in normal life. It can feel awkward to stand one foot away from someone when normally you'd be two or two-and-a-half feet away. It's an interesting illusion caused by the camera lens. The two-shot is used more in film because it shows as much as a close-up does on television. Television usually considers it rather static and not detailed enough.

Over-the-Shoulder ■   Technically, the over-the-shoulder angle is a two-person shot because two characters are in the shot—one character is in a medium close-up and framed by the other character's head and shoulder. This is a bread-and-butter shot for both TV and film. The camera, however, is now close enough to cause precise restrictions on the actor's movements. And the restrictions are placed on both the actor facing the camera and the actor with his back toward the lens.

The actor facing the camera has little margin for error in movement from side to side because with just a small move (shifting weight from leg to leg) he will either bump into the frame on one side or be blocked by the other actor's head on the other side. He also has to make sure that he stays in his light (very specifically placed) and doesn't go into the shadow caused by the other actor's head.

On the other hand, the actor with his back to the camera has to be aware of two problems: first, he can't move too much or he will ruin the shot by either blocking the actor in close-up or going

Over-the-Shoulder

Close-up

out of frame, and second, he can't remain stiff because, as the director cuts back and forth from character to character, the actor will not match his behavior on his own close-up. It sounds awkward, but after a while it all becomes second nature. The important thing is to be aware of the hidden traps.

Close-up ■   This is *the* shot of the soap-opera crew. They love the close-up and must use it 80 percent of the time. Films have to be very careful because this shot can be too overpowering on those huge screens. The framing of the close-up (CU) can range from a medium close-up (bust), two-button (the bottom of the frame aligns with the second button of your shirt) to an ECU or extreme close-up (just your face or eyes). Obviously, the actor in a close-up has to be acutely aware of his movements. And here is where craft is important: knowing how to avoid being restricted and stiff, how to stay as alive and free physically as you did in the master and two-shot, and how to avoid bumping into the frame and ruining the take in the close-up.

Egocentric actors love the close-up. I had an editor tell me about a big name actor on a hit TV series who would call him up, yelling and screaming, "You SOB! You keep cutting away from my close-up to go back to the master! I keep telling you that I do my best work in my close-ups!" Enough said.

Depending on the complexity of the production, there are other technical shots, but these are the basic shot angles and actors should be constantly aware of what kind of shot they're dealing with and react accordingly. When the director is blocking, I'm already thinking about coverage so that I can anticipate where the over-the-shoulders and close-ups will be, staying physically simple and clean around those moments.

During the blocking period the director will also indicate any physical business he wants you to do (washing dishes, mixing a drink, bandaging another character's arm). He usually won't tell you exactly how to wash each dish or in what sequence to do it. He will probably say something like, "After you get to the sink, I want you to start washing the dishes. When you hear your husband say, '*We're going to settle this now Beth!*' I want you to stop washing, turn to Bill with a dish in your hand and say your line: '*I can't Bill. Not right now, right now I'm going to wash this dish. If you want to help me wash this dish, you're welcome to but I am going to wash the dishes and that's all.*' When Bill doesn't do anything, I want you to quietly let the dish slide from your hand and crash to the floor. You then walk out of the kitchen."

After the blocking period you will have time to set a sequence of how you wash the dishes so that you can do the scene from any angle and match your takes. But the primary responsibility to improvise the action first and then set it is yours.

Rehearsal

Immediately after the director has finished blocking he will say, "OK everybody, let's try it. First positions!"—which indicates the first mark you were given at the beginning of the scene. You have to be ready that quickly to play the scene. This could be the only run-through you will have so make the most of it. Remember, up to this point you only have your lines learned and your tentative choices made. Now you're adding the blocking. You still don't know how the other actor(s) will play the scene, so be ready to be spontaneous and open to what is happening around you. Be ready to *adjust* moment to moment. Once the actors are on their first mark, the director gives "Action." Although the blocking is unfamiliar, try the best you can to hit your marks but keep your concentration on your ultimate goal and that is the character's behavior. Once the director says "Action," you are only thinking and feeling as the character. I can't stress this enough. The director is expecting a performance-level run-through here. It's the first time he has seen your work (your choices) and he needs to see if the scene now works. If it doesn't, he has to fix it. So you can't give him a "walk through" of the scene while you work on the blocking, you have to play the scene fully.

Sometimes the director will stop in the middle of the scene to adjust the blocking and sometimes he may even walk on the set and move you to a new position even as the scene continues. Don't lose your concentration, just keep going and stay *in* the scene. Remember also that this run-through is practice for the camera operators and the sound crew. Everyone has a stake in this rehearsal.

Lighting Time

Once you hear the director say, "Cut!" he will ask all the tech guys if everything worked for their needs. If all is satisfactory, the director will turn the set over to the lighting crew so they can prepare the lights for the first shot. Lighting is one of the most important technical aspects of the film medium. The story is told with visual images and the lighting creates the look of those images. It is also the most laborious and time-consuming of the technical disciplines. It can take anywhere from minutes to many, many hours to get the set ready to shoot.

The good news is that this is the time to take advantage of that gap in time. The bad news is that everybody else seems to want a piece of you too. Wardrobe, makeup, and hair all need to freshen you up for the master shot. Usually, however, there will be time for your own preparation. This period of time is extremely valuable because, where before all your choices were tentative, you now have experienced all the variables. You know any script changes, the blocking, the other actor's choices and, most importantly, the director has given his approval of your work (choices) on the scene. In a few minutes (or hours) you will shoot the master. By the time it is shot, the master should become just another shot.

Since you *do not* shoot the master first and then try to remember what you did in order to shoot other angles, this post-blocking period means time to go back to your script and notes and *set* all your choices. Knowing the blocking moves, you can also adjust your speakout to cover any pauses that you hadn't planned for. You have the responsibility to justify your character's actions during the scene. The director told Beth to hold the plate out and let it slip from her hand—you have to justify that behavior with motivation. That motivation is in your objectives, subtext, and emotions: your choices. So go to work!

Some directors who like to work with their actors, squeezing any time they can to rehearse, might take advantage of this period to gather the actors together and review the scene. It doesn't happen that often in television but quite often in film, especially with critical scenes. If the director doesn't want to rehearse, the other actor(s), who previously weren't interested, may be now begging to work on the scene.

When the First AD originally called you for the scene, he probably yelled something like, "OK, scene 43, let's have the first team please!" The principle actors in the scene are the first team—that means you. When the director is finished with the blocking, the First AD usually yells, "Let's have the second team!"—those are the stand-ins. They are extras (atmosphere people) hired to watch the blocking and then stand on the various marks so that the camera crew can adjust their focus and the lighting people can set their lights. They aren't there because you're a big star and can't be bothered; it's a hot and tiring experience that can wilt makeup and sap your energy. You need to use the time for preparation.

Sometimes, however, I will ask to take the place of my stand-in so that I can get on the set and "make the blocking my own." This is especially true of scenes where there is quite a bit of movement and use of props. The director has given me all these moves, marks to hit, props to use and extra improvised moments I need to get comfortable with and *set* just as I did my choices. The only way to do this is to get on the set and practice. But when you do replace a stand-in, it is with the understanding that if the cameraman or lighting person needs you on a mark or to make a move, you've got to be there for them.

Relaxation

Along about now you will begin to feel an icy creep of realization that you are about to do this thing for real. And when that happens, nerves begin to act up. This is a great time to do some relaxation exercises. I hope you've got a good relaxation technique available because, at some time or other, you will need it.

The problem sometimes arises when the technique you use (say lying or sitting down and doing yoga or TM) becomes unusable; when, for example, during the shoot, you are on your mark, ready for a close-up of an important moment, and you feel tension attack your body. There's no time to leave the set and lay down. This can be a major problem because the whole concept of "inside-out" work is that your instrument (body and voice) must be free enough to allow the internal work (subtext and emotions) to motivate real behavior. When you get overly tense, the system just doesn't work, so you need a relaxation technique that works within the confines of a working set. I use a tense-release relaxation method based on "centers of residual tension," which I learned from my work with Lee Strasberg. It has worked in the past and I trust it, but the operative word here is trust.

I've learned any number of personal relaxation tricks from various friends and co-actors. One technique is to carry a dime or quarter with you, and when the old nerves start kicking up, you just take out the coin and concentrate totally on it. Look at the minute scratches on it, notice the patina and color, study the face of Washington or Roosevelt. In a matter of seconds, you will feel yourself slowly release the tension. It can work beautifully. The important thing is to have something available—for psychological security, if nothing else. Trusting that you will relax when you need to often works better than the technique itself. The reality is that the origin of most tension for the actor comes from psychological causes. The time limitations create incredible pressure, and pressure creates tension. It then follows that any relaxation technique should involve psychological keys that can affect those causes.

On Set

Finally the First AD yells, "OK everyone, first team!" The director will then make the decision to do another run-through to rehearse both his actors and the camera moves. This is particularly true for scenes involving a lot of moves, action, or especially stunts. Most stunts, particularly the dangerous ones, are blocked and rehearsed in the most minute detail to ensure the greatest safety for the actors and the stunt people. But for the average television scene, the director usually decides to "shoot the rehearsal." His thinking is, "Why waste a possibly good take on a rehearsal?" It saves time and any cost of film, if the take is unusable, is negligible. To the actor, it translates to no rehearsal. You're called back to the set, the director says, "Let's shoot this turkey . . . First positions!" and you're about to shoot the master.

Roll Camera

The technical procedure for a one-camera shot that actually starts the filming of a scene has a definite chronological sequence to it. After the actors are on first positions, the First AD takes over and controls the process with a set of commands:

1. "Quiet on the set, please! . . . Put us on a bell."
   This means the sound man (usually) is in control of a little box that turns off the air-conditioning system, turns on blinking red lights inside and outside of the thick soundproof doors of the soundstages, and rings a bell or buzzer that allows everyone inside the soundstage to know the shooting has started and absolute quiet is needed. If you are anywhere on that soundstage and hear one bell, don't make a sound until you hear two bells which is the all clear sound.
2. "Roll camera!"
   The camera operator turns on the camera, and when it gets up to speed (24 frames per second) he yells, "Camera rolling!" At the same time, the sound person turns on the voice-tape recorder and yells, "Speed!" Now the First AD knows he has film and sound going.
3. "Mark!"
   Another tech person will then hold a clap board (small blackboard with a hinged stick attached) up in front of you saying, "Scene 43 apple, take one!" He then claps the sticks together and backs off. This procedure allows the editor to later sync the film and the sound together. There is only one frame of the twenty-four frames per second where the sticks come together and only one place on the audio tape where the clapping sound occurs. Load the film and the tape into an editing machine and sound and film are in sync.
   The director now takes over.
4. "Action!"
   Your cue to begin the action of the scene. Do not start before action and do not stop before you hear "cut."

   That is the basic sequence you will hear, give or take idiosyn-
cratic personal preferences. I take the time to describe the process
because during this sequence, you have your own process going
on that is extremely important. During that 20 to 25 seconds you
have to get into your pre-shoot program. Remember all the work
done on opening objective and opening emotion? By the time the
director is ready to say "Action!" you should already have level
two (subtext) and level three (emotions) working for you. You
don't begin the actual behavior or action of the scene until
"Action!" but you definitely *be*come the character. I can't stress
how important this time interval is to starting the scene correctly.
   Once the director gives the "Action!" command, you begin the
scripted and blocked behavior of the scene. Once started, do not
break or stop the scene for any reason. In the master, especially,
the director knows he will only use certain portions of the shot,
so if you bobble a line or don't hit a mark perfectly, keep going.
The only person allowed to interrupt a shot is the director. He
may very well stop a scene in the middle and say, "Let's go back
to the beginning." He may even keep the cameras rolling while
the actors go back to their first positions. It happens all the time
in sitcoms. On "Cheers," director Jimmy Burrows knew what he
wanted in every beat, every run of the scenes—so well that if a
line was missed or the timing off for just a split second, he often
would tell the crew to keep the cameras rolling and go back to
such and such a line. In situations like this you must keep your
concentration, stay in character, forget whatever went wrong,
and fight to get level two and three going again.
   The opposite is also true in stopping a scene. Don't stop your
character's behavior until the director says, "Cut!" Many times the
director will need a number of extra frames for a fade-out or a
cross fade. He may not tell you beforehand, so you get to the end
of the scene as written and directed, and the director has not said,
"Cut." You have to continue the character's behavior. The only
way to do this is to sustain the character's thoughts and emotions.
You see this happen in the end of soap-opera scenes all the time.
   The director may shoot the master two or three times or
maybe only once. Once the director is satisfied, he may say, "Print
takes two and three," and he will go on to shoot coverage. If
you've done your preparation properly, you won't be worrying
about remembering what you did in the master or about matching in the upcoming shots.
   The next shot angle depends on many technical decisions—
you could be immediately faced with a close-up from any part the

scene. Very infrequently will the director shoot a complete take of a close-up from beginning to end unless it is a short intimate scene with very little movement. They shoot small segments of a scene from different angles and often out of chronological order. For the actors, that means they have to keep their concentration in focus, adjust to circumstances quickly, and be ready for several stops and starts. You will be programming and reprogramming your computer constantly, making good use of instant believability technique. It is imperative that you be able to release the emotions of the character after a take and get back to the opening emotions used at the beginning of each take. The greater the emotional intensity of the transitions in any given shot, the greater the difficulty in releasing those emotions.

It's a Wrap

Eventually, after he has covered all his angles, the director will say, "Print it, let's go to the next scene!" and your scene is finished. If you've got other scenes to shoot, it's hurry up and wait all over again. If not, "it's a wrap" and the Second AD comes up to you, sticks a sign-out form in front of your face, and your day on the set is over.

It will have been a tiring but exhilarating day. If you have prepared well and kept your concentration, then you will walk away feeling like you have accomplished something that you can be proud of—whether it was a starring role in a major feature film or a walk-on in the most banal episodic television show. Good craft, believability, and emotional truth have value in any genre, any medium, on any level. The work must stand for itself. Late one cold December night twenty years later, as you sit in front of your aging television set, your old performance might come flickering across the screen, and you will smile to yourself and think, "I did good work that day." To say less is to admit neglect, to say more is always our fondest desire. I wish you that good craftsmanship so that the talent inside of you can find expression.

Epilogue

Over the years I have led many actors through the transitional material you have just worked on. I tell everyone the same thing: "What we are doing is not brain surgery." It is technical and challenging, but it is not unattainable. It is a matter of understanding, of practice, of experience, ultimately, a matter of craft. As Sir Anthony Hopkins said, "It's about balance, finally it's about making a film, it's not that important." Craft can be learned. Talent is another story.

Many times actors have come up to me after seminars around the country and asked, "Am I good enough to move to New York or Los Angeles?" I advise them all in the same way, "Nobody should tell you to act and nobody should tell you not to. If you have to act, you will. Otherwise, maybe you shouldn't." Our profession is probably the least secure on the face of the earth. It offers the highest rewards with, statistically, the lowest number reaping those rewards. Still it never has been a question of money, it has always been about the doing. I hope we can all retain and harbor that small spark of idealism for our art. Someone once said, and it has become my favorite definition of art, "Art is art only at the moment of utterance." Acting in front of an audience or the camera, is about that moment. The difference is that your audience in theatre is numbered in the thousands while the screen reaches millions.

Appendix A

A
Abandon
Abdicate
Abduct
Abhor
Abolish
Abort
Abscond
Absolve
Absorb
Abstain
Abuse
Accede
Accelerate
Accept
Acclaim
Acclimate
Accommodate
Accomplish
Account
Accumulate
Accuse
Ace
Acerbate
Achieve
Acknowledge
Acquiesce
Acquire
Act

Activate
Adapt
Admire
Admit
Admonish
Adore
Absorb
Adulate
Advance
Advise
Advocate
Affect
Affirm
Aggrandize
Aggravate
Aggress
Agitate
Agonize
Alarm
Alert
Alibi
Alleviate
Amaze
Ambush
Amend
Amplify
Amuse
Analyze
Anesthetize

Anger
Anguish
Animate
Annihilate
Annoy
Antagonize
Anticipate
Apologize
Appeal
Appease
Appose
Appraise
Appreciate
Apprehend
Apprise
Approach
Approve
Arbitrate
Argue
Arouse
Arrest
Articulate
Aspire
Assail
Assault
Assert
Assist
Assuage
Assure

125

Astonish
Astound
Atone
Attack
Attend
Attract
Avail
Avert
Avoid
Await
Awake

B
Back
Backbite
Bad-mouth
Baffle
Bait
Bamboozle
Bandy
Banish
Banter
Bargain
Barter
Bawl
Bear
Bedazzle
Bedevil
Befoul
Befriend
Befuddle
Beg
Begrudge
Beguile
Believe
Beleaguer
Belittle
Bemuse
Bend
Benefit
Berate
Beseech
Beset
Besiege
Bespeak
Bestow
Betray
Bewilder
Bewitch
Blame
Blandish
Bluff

Bolster
Bombard
Boost
Bother
Bribe
Browbeat
Brutalize
Bully
Butter up

C
Cajole
Calm
Capture
Castigate
Cater
Censure
Challenge
Charge
Charm
Chasten
Chastise
Cheat
Cherish
Chide
Clarify
Coax
Coddle
Coerce
Collaborate
Comfort
Command
Commend
Commiserate
Commit
Commune
Compel
Compete
Compliment
Con
Concern
Concede
Conciliate
Concur
Condemn
Condole
Condone
Confer
Confess
Confound
Confront
Confuse

Confute
Console
Contest
Contradict
Control
Convince
Corner
Correct
Corrupt
Counteract
Cow
Cramp
Criticize
Cross-examine
Cultivate
Curtail

D
Damn
Dare
Daunt
Daze
Dazzle
Debate
Deceive
Declare
Defame
Defend
Deflate
Defraud
Defy
Defuse
Degrade
Delight
Demean
Demoralize
Denigrate
Denounce
Deny
Deplore
Deprecate
Depreciate
Deride
Deprive
Describe
Desire
Despise
Detest
Detract
Devalue
Disapprove
Disarm

Disbelieve
Discompose
Disconcert
Discourage
Discredit
Disdain
Disgrace
Dishearten
Dishonor
Disillusion
Dismay
Dismiss
Disorient
Dispirit
Dispute
Disquiet
Disregard
Dissuade
Distract
Distress
Disturb
Divert
Dodge
Dominate
Doom
Dote
Doubt
Dread
Drive
Dupe

E
Edify
Elate
Embarrass
Enchant
Encourage
Endorse
Endure
Engross
Enjoin
Enliven
Entertain
Entice
Entreat
Escape
Examine
Excite
Exclude
Exonerate
Explore
Expose

Express
Extol

F
Familiarize
Fault
Finagle
Flatter
Fish
Flay
Flog
Flirt
Fluster
Forbid
Force
Forewarn
Forgive
Frighten
Frustrate

G
Galvanize
Gibe
Glorify
Grant
Greet
Guide

H
Hail
Haggle
Hamper
Harass
Harry
Hate
Heckle
Henpeck
Honor
Humble
Humiliate
Hurry
Hush
Hustle

I
Identify
Idolize
Ignore
Implicate
Implore
Impress
Impugn

Incite
Incriminate
Indict
Induce
Indulge
Inflict
Influence
Inform
Infuriate
Ingrain
Ingratiate
Inhibit
Initiate
Injure
Inquire
Insinuate
Insist
Inspect
Inspire
Instigate
Instruct
Insulate
Insult
Intercede
Intercept
Interest
Interfere
Interpret
Interrupt
Intervene
Interview
Intimidate
Intoxicate
Intrigue
Introduce
Intrude
Inundate
Invalidate
Invent
Investigate
Invite
Involve
Irritate
Isolate

J
Jab
Jam
Jeer
Jest
Jilt
Jog

Joggle
Judge

K
Keep
Kid
Kill
Kindle
Kiss
Knock

L
Label
Lambaste
Lampoon
Last
Laud
Laze
Lead
Leak
Lean
Level
Liberate
Lie
Like
Limit
Link
Liven
Loathe
Locate
Love
Lull
Lure
Lust
Luxuriate

M
Magnify
Malign
Manage
Manipulate
Mark
Marry
Mask
Master
Meander
Mediate
Menace
Mend
Minimize
Minister
Mislead

Mislike
Mistrust
Mock
Moderate
Modify
Mold
Mollify
Monitor
Mooch
Moralize
Motivate
Mourn
Mull
Murder
Muse

N
Nail
Nag
Neutralize
Nose
Note
Notice
Notify
Nurture
Numb

O
Obfuscate
Object
Obligate
Oblige
Obscure
Observe
Obstruct
Offend
Offer
Operate
Oppose
Organize
Ostracize
Oust
Outclass
Outrage
Outwit
Overrule
Overwhelm

P
Pacify
Pamper
Pan

Pander
Pardon
Parry
Participate
Party
Patronize
Penetrate
Perceive
Perfect
Perform
Permit
Perplex
Persecute
Persist
Persuade
Pester
Petition
Pillory
Pitch
Pity
Placate
Plead
Pleasure
Pledge
Ponder
Possess
Praise
Preach
Prejudice
Prefer
Prepare
Pressure
Present
Press
Pretend
Prevail
Prevent
Prime
Prize
Probe
Process
Proclaim
Procure
Produce
Profess
Profit
Prohibit
Promise
Promote
Prompt
Propose
Proposition

Prosecute
Protect
Protest
Prove
Provide
Provoke
Pry
Publicize
Pump
Punish
Pursuade
Pursue

Q
Qualify
Quarrel
Quash
Query
Question
Quiet
Quip
Quit

R
Race
Rag
Rage
Raise
Rally
Ram
Rationalize
Rattle
Ravage
Rave
React
Reason
Reassure
Rebel
Rebuff
Rebuke
Rebut
Recede
Reciprocate
Recognize
Recommend
Reconcile
Recover
Recruit
Rectify
Recriminate
Redeem
Reduce

Refine
Reflect
Reform
Refuse
Refute
Regale
Regulate
Rehash
Reiterate
Reject
Rejoice
Rejoin
Relate
Relax
Release
Relent
Relish
Rely
Remember
Remind
Remove
Repel
Repent
Repress
Reprimand
Reproach
Reprove
Repudiate
Repulse
Request
Rescue
Resent
Resist
Resolve
Respect
Respond
Rest
Restore
Restrain
Resume
Retaliate
Retreat
Retrieve
Reveal
Revenge
Revere
Review
Revile
Revise
Revive
Revolt
Reward

Rib
Rid
Ridicule
Right
Rob
Rouse
Rue
Ruin
Rule
Rummage
Run
Rush

S
Sacrifice
Sanction
Satiate
Satirize
Satisfy
Savage
Scan
Scandalize
Scare
Scathe
Schmooze
Scoff
Scold
Score
Scorn
Scout
Scramble
Screen
Screw
Scrutinize
Search
Secure
Seduce
Seek
Seize
Sense
Shame
Shield
Silence
Simplify
Slander
Slight
Slur
Smear
Snare
Snitch
Snub
Soothe

Spellbind
Spite
Spoof
Spoon
Spot
Spur
Spurn
Spy
Stabilize
Stand by
Steady
Stifle
Stigmatize
Stimulate
Stir
Stroke
Stultify
Stun
Stupefy
Subdue
Subvert
Sue
Summon
Supplicate
Support
Surpass
Surprise
Suspect
Sustain
Swindle
Sympathize

T
Tame
Taunt
Tax
Teach
Tease
Tempt
Terrify
Test
Threaten
Thrill
Thwart
Titillate
Tolerate
Torment
Tranquilize
Trap
Treasure
Trick
Trifle

Trouble
Trust
Try
Tutor
Twist

U
Unburden
Uncover
Undermine
Unmask
Unite
Unload
Unnerve
Unsettle
Uphold
Uplift
Upset
Urge
Use

V
Validate
Venerate
Vent
Venture
Verbalize
Vex
Vilify
Vindicate
Vitalize
Voice
Volunteer
Vow

W
Wander
Wangle
Warn
Welcome
Win
Wing it
Withdraw
Withstand
Witness
Woo
Work
Worship
Wrangle
Wreck
Wrestle

Y
Yank
Yield

Z
Zone out

Appendix B

Glossary of Film and Television Terms

"Action": The verbal cue indicating the camera is rolling and actors should begin.

AD: The assistant director, directly responsible to the director and for maintaining optimum coordination of cast and crew.

Ad Agency: An agency where the concepts for and writing of commercials takes place; the actual production/filming is sub-contracted to production houses.

Adjustment: 1. A change in the actor's choices made by the actor or the director. 2. A change in pay brought about under certain circumstances to compensate the actor for work not covered by his normal pay.

AFTRA: American Federation of Television & Radio Artists. The union that represents performers (including newscasters and announcers) in live and taped TV shows, radio spots, recordings, and videotaped commercials and industrials.

Agent: The actor's representative. A talent agent approved by AFTRA or SAG to solicit and negotiate employment for their members. Must sign a contract with the appropriate union, thus becoming "franchised." If an agent isn't franchised, s/he isn't "legit;" s/he can't negotiate the actor's contracts with union productions, nor can s/he take a commission.

Audition: A tryout for a role, in front of a casting director, director, or client, for which a reading or improvisation is required.

Availability: Inquiry by the producer to see if you are free for a particular day or time period to do a job.

Atmosphere: Extras or performers best described as part of the background.

"Background Action": A direction for extras or atmosphere to begin their action before action is called for the principal actors.

131

Best Boy: Assistant electrician directly responsible to the head electrician or **gaffer**.

Blocking: The physical movements given by the director for actors to perform in any scene.

Booking: A firm commitment to a performer to do a specific job. "I'd like to book you for this job. The booking is for this date. Consider yourself booked."

Boom: A mobile, cranelike device to which the microphone is attached during the filming process.

Breakdown: A detailed listing and description of roles available for casting in a production.

Buyout: Payment to an extra or hand model for a session fee with no residual payments required.

Business: The onstage actions and movements of performers, or specific aspects of these, during a scene.

Call: The exact time that an actor is to report to the set for work.

Callback: Any follow-up interview or audition after the initial audition.

Call Sheet: A sheet given to each member of the cast and crew at the end of each day's work with the next day's shooting schedule, call times, and other pertinent information.

Casting Director: A person or agency contracted by a client to bring in actors to audition for the client's project. The casting director is hired by and is working for the client, not the actor.

Casting Call: A session in which actors are brought in to audition for a project. Casting calls are held by advertising agencies, producers, and casting directors.

Cheat: The regrouping or rearrangement of performers or props in relationship to the background or each other for the purpose of changing the angle of view.

Cheat Your Look: A specific direction to the actor to angle his head to the left or right (or up or down) for better camera coverage of his face.

Clean Entrance/Clean Exit: For a clean entrance the actor must start completely off camera or out of frame and enter the scene. For a clean exit, he must move completely out of frame at the point he is directed to do so.

Client: The company that contracts to have a job done.

Close-up (or **CU**): A camera angle that will show only the actor's face or, in an extreme close-up, only the eyes or mouth.

Cold Reading: An unrehearsed reading of a scene at auditions.

Commercial Exclusivity or Conflict: A regulation which prohibits a principal player in a specific commercial, from accepting a job in a commercial for a competing product for as long as that player is being held on the first commercial. (If you have a Coke commercial running, you can't do Pepsi; if you are in a Purity Supreme ad you can't do Stop and Shop, etc. A product can also be a company, like Filene's or Black & Decker.)

Commission: The percentage of a performer's earnings paid to agents or managers for services rendered. Only franchised agents are allowed to take a commission. (See **scale plus 10 percent**.)

Composite: Several contrasting photos (usually four) on the back with actor's head shot on the front. Usually used for commercial auditions.

Copy: The script for a radio or TV commercial. Also used loosely to refer to any writing for TV or radio.

Coverage: The filming from different angles of the same scene.

Critical Mark: A mark that an actor must hit in order to be in frame and/or focus.

CSA: Casting Society of America, an organization for casting directors.

Cue: A verbal or physical signal to tell talent or crew when to proceed with action.

Cue Card: A large poster-sized card with copy written on it in large letters, used mostly at auditions and sometimes for on-air programs.

Cut: Any deletion from the original script. Also the order to the actors and/or technicians to stop action.

Dailies (also called **Rushes**): The processed results of the previous day's photographic efforts.

Day Player: A principal performer hired on a daily basis, rather than on a longer term contract.

Dealer Spot/Commercial: A national commercial produced and paid for by a national advertiser and then turned over to local dealers to book airtime, usually with a dealer's tag added on.

Deferred payment: An agreement to work without payment with the understanding that payment will be delayed (not waived) until the project generates income. Deferred payment must be approved by the union.

Demo (also called **Reel**): An audition tape or a client demo commercial for which payment must be made.

Depth Of Field: The distance in front of and behind the subject in which detail remains in acceptable focus.

Dialogue: The words spoken by performers during the filming process.

Director: The supervisor of production and the person responsible for bringing the script to life on film.

Director of Photography (or **DP**): The person directly responsible to the director and who assists the director in translating the screenplay into visual images; supervises all lighting of a scene.

Dissolve: Fading action out of one scene into another.

Dolly: A wheeled mount for moving the camera from one position to another.

Double: An individual, similar in build and coloring, who takes the place of a principal during the filming of a scene when an element of danger exists or when special abilities are needed.

Double Time: Double the straight time pay which is payable for certain overtime hours defined in each contract.

Downgrade: To hire a performer as principal in a commercial and move her or him to a lower category. When a performer is engaged as a principal but her or his voice does not remain in the commercial as exhibited, the performer must be notified that s/he has been downgraded. This means no residuals will be forthcoming, but the actor will receive one additional session fee.

Dress the set: Add items to the set such as curtains, furniture, props, etc.

8-by-10: A commonly used size for photos of headshots and for composites.

Dubbing: A process of combining sound recordings into one master recording or the process in which new dialogue is recorded and substituted for the original dialogue.

Editor: The person responsible for the postproduction or completion of the film or videotape production; that is, the proper arrangement of scenes and the synchronization of all sound and picture elements that will appear in the release prints of the film.

Establishing Shot: A wide camera shot that orients the audience as to location.

Executive Producer: The person responsible for funding the production.

Exteriors: Scenes for TV or motion pictures taken outdoors or using outdoor sets in a studio.

Extra: A nonprincipal role, used as background. Also called **atmosphere** or **background**.

Extreme Close-up (**ECU**): Very tight shot of a subject (actor's eyes/bird's beak).

Fill: Area lighting that "fills in" **Key Lighting**.

First Refusal: A request by a producer to hold a particular date open for a job. If you receive another job offer for that date, tell the second producer you're on first refusal and you'll get back to him/her. Then call the first producer and ask if he/she is going to use you. If the answer is yes, you're booked with the first producer; if it is no, you can take the second booking.

First Team: In movies, the stars and principals; actors with lines; the principal performers in a scene, as opposed to the **Second Team** which is composed of **Stand-ins**.

Fitting Charge: An extra payment for actors when they are required to report to the studio or elsewhere in advance of the actual work date for wardrobe fittings.

First: Short for **First Assistant Director**.

Fixed Cycle: For commercials, an established 13-week period for which the advertiser pays a holding fee to retain the right to use the commercial. The first fixed cycle starts with your session date.

Forced Call: When an actor is called to report to the set the next day without having had his full 12-hour rest period or **Turnaround Period** between calls; **Adjustments** in salary are due.

Frame Line: The line framing what is actually being photographed.

Gaffer: The electrician responsible for lighting the stage.

"Give Me a Level": A direction given to adjust sound equipment for proper recording. The sound man will direct a performer to do this. It means to start speaking as if you're actually performing.

Glossy: A shiny photofinishing process; also a term which means an 8-by-10 photo.

Golden Time: Double time paid after ten hours of work (whereas overtime is paid at the rate of time-and-a-half).

Grips: The individuals who work with studio equipment on the set; laborers.

Having Had: A term used on a call sheet, meaning to report to the set "having had" your breakfast, lunch, or dinner, depending on the time of your call.

Heads: Slang for close-ups.

Headshot (also **Headsheet**): A photo, usually 8-by-10, of the actor's head and shoulders.

Hold: A hold is the same as a booking. It is an offer of employment—a verbal contract—and is binding. Some people use the term as if it meant **First Refusal**, which is inappropriate. If unsure, always ask, "Do you mean that I am firmly booked for this job on this date?"

Holding Fee: A fee paid to the actor that gives the producer the right to hold and show the commercial in which an actor appears. The holding fee is the same amount as one session fee (unless otherwise negotiated) and is paid at the beginning of each 13-week period (called a cycle) for as long as the commercial is being held by the agency or producer. The session fee covers the first 13-week holding fee.

Honey Wagon: A tractor-trailer truck with numerous small cubicles used as dressing room and bath rooms..

Hot Set: A set which is in use and should not be disturbed in any way.

IATSE: International Alliance of Theatrical and Stage Employees. A union including craftsmen and technicians.

Improvisation (Improv): A situation given to the actors by the director in which they create dialogue and/or actions. Frequently done in auditions when there is no actor copy for a commercial. Additional fees may be required under various contracts.

Industrial: Nonbroadcast, often educational, films or tapes designed for in-house use by a company. Also called Corporate Video.

"IN" Time: An actor's call or start time; also return time from lunch or dinner break.

Key Grip: Head **Grip**. Responsible for crew.

Key Light: The main light source lighting an actor.

"Lay it down": A direction to record or film the material.

Long Shot (LS): A camera shot which captures the actor's whole body.

Lines: The actor's dialogue in the script.

Location: Anywhere other than the studio where filming is designated.

Looping: Also called line replaccment or dubbing. A process for replacing the sound track recorded during the filming process with a new sound track that is recorded under studio conditions. This process is done on an ADR stage—Automatic Dialogue Recording.

Major markets: Large cities where the majority of work takes place. Los Angeles and New York are the two largest.

Mark: The spot, usually indicated by tape, where an actor is assigned to stand.

Master: The main and most general shot of a scene being filmed.

Master Shot: A wide camera shot of the complete scene, to be intercut with close-ups, etc.

Matching: Performing the same actions and the same behavior at the same point in time in each take during the filming of a scene.

Meal Penalty: An adjustment assessed over and above an actor's salary when he or she is not released for a meal after a certain number of hours of work.

Medium Close-Up (MCU): A camera shot that is not as tight as a close-up.

Medium Shot (MS): A closer shot than a long shot.

Mixer: An individual who operates the sound recording equipment.

MOS: Without sound. When a scene is shot and no sound track is recorded.

Multicamera: More than one camera used during filming.

National Commercial: A commercial aired nationwide.

Night Premium: A percentage surcharge for work performed between 8:00 P.M. and 6:00 A.M.

Off-camera (**OC** or **Off-screen** or **Voice-over**): Dialogue delivered without being on screen.

Open Call: An audition or interview situation open to anyone.

"OUT" time: The time after which you have changed out of wardrobe and are released.

Overtime (**OT**): Work extending beyond eight hours.

Over the Shoulder: A shot over the shoulder of one actor to the face of another.

PA: Production assistant. Worker on a set who does whatever is assigned to him or her (directing traffic, rounding up extras, keeping onlookers out of picture, etc.).

Pan: A horizontal movement of the camera from one point of the set to another.

Paymaster: An independent talent payment company that provides a payroll service for signatories and acts as the employer of record. For the industrial contract, the paymaster may also be the signatory.

Per Diem: Money paid directly to the actor while on location to cover meals and miscellaneous expenses.

Peripheral Vision: Seeing from the corners of your eyes; used for hitting marks and knowing where the camera is without looking at it.

Pick-up: An added shot, either in the normal course of coverage or when a portion of a take must be re-shot.

Pilot: A first film or videotape production for a potential series.

Postproduction: Everything that takes place on a TV show, movie, or commercial after shooting is done. Music, voice-over, sound effects, editing, etc.

POV: Point of view.

Preproduction: Everything that takes place on a TV show, movie, or commercial before shooting begins. Casting, location scouting, script, etc.

Principal: An actor who is given a scripted line or lines or is asked to speak and is recorded during filming. Some contracts (industrial/commercial) also provide for performers to be paid as principals under other specific conditions.

Producer: Often called the Line Producer; the person from the production company responsible for the day-to-day decision making on a production. Concerned with administrative details.

PSA: Public Service Announcement. A spot for a nonprofit organization, a not-for-profit-fund-raising event, a charity, etc. Actors are usually paid a session fee but no residuals for doing a PSA. A waiver must be granted by the union to the producer prior to employment.

"Print": A good take, one that will be printed at the lab for viewing .

Process: Any of several methods used for photographing foreground subject matter in front of a background that was previously filmed.

Reaction shot: A shot taken of an actor responding to another actor's lines or actions. Frequently done independently of the action.

Regional Commercial (or **Regional**): A commercial produced for airing only in certain areas of the U.S., not nationwide.

Rerun: A rebroadcast of a TV program.

Residual: The fee paid to a performer for rebroadcast of a commercial, film, or TV program.

Resume: A list of credits, usually attached to the back of an 8-by-10 **Headshot**.

Retakes: Shooting the same scene over again due to a technical or acting error.

Reuse: Rebroadcast of a commercial.

Reverse: A camera angle description. If your face is featured in one shot, the reverse will feature the other actor's face.

Revisions: Script changes.

Run-Through: A prefilming rehearsal of the scene.

Rushes: See **Dailies**.

SAG: Screen Actors Guild; the actor's union.

Scale: The minimum amount of money the SAG allows an actor to be paid.

Scale +10 percent: A minimum payment plus 10 percent generally charged to cover an agent's commission; required in some jurisdictions for agents to receive commissions.

Scene numbers: Numbers found in the margins of the script pages. Each scene is numbered in the shooting script.

Script Supervisor: The person mainly responsible for checking dialogue during filming. The script supervisor also keeps a record of the filmed scenes, and checks continuity with respect to wardrobe, props, and action.

Second Team: The stand-ins who take the actor's place on the marks during the technical prepping for a scene.

Shooting Schedule: A schedule showing exactly what scenes will be shot each day along with where and when they will be shot and the cast involved.

Slate: A small board upon which the scene number, take number, production number and name, director's name, and date are written. This is held in front of the camera and photographed before a scene is filmed. The hinged clapper is slapped and the clapping noise on the sound track synchronizes the film and track for the editor.

Slop Over: Slang meaning that the day's work was not completed and will slop over to the next day.

"Speed": A term used by operators of film, video, or sound equipment to indicate equipment has reached the proper RPMs and is ready to record.

Spokesperson/Spokes: An on- or off-camera performer speaking as him/herself directly to the viewing/listening audience.

Spot: A commercial message.

Standard Union Contract: The contract approved by AFTRA/SAG, completed by the producer and performer at the time of a shoot and submitted for payment.

"Stand by": An order to get ready to begin given by director, assistant director, production assistants.

Stand-in: An extra player used to substitute for featured players, usually for the purpose of setting lights, camera blocking, etc.

Step Into: A term meaning the actor starts the scene completely off-camera and moves into frame.

Storyboard: An artist's hand-drawn rendering of each camera setup.

Studio: A building which accommodates film or TV production.

Submission: The presentation of an actor's **headshot** to a **producer** for consideration for an audition or a role, usually by an agent or casting director.

Swing Into: A term meaning the actor has one foot on a mark, but his body is out of frame. On the word "Action" the actor pivots on that foot and swings into the frame.

Taft Hartley: The provision in the Screen Actors Guild Agreement that allows a person to work once in a production or commercial and not join the union. This provision is applicable only when certain conditions of employment exist.

Take: A shot being filmed.

Talent: Anyone who appears on camera or whose voice is heard as voice-over.

TelePrompTer: A device which scrolls a script, enabling the performer to read while appearing to know or to have memorized the material.

Tight Shot: Framing of a shot with little or no space around the central figure(s) or features(s); usually a close-up.

Theatrical: TV shows or feature film work, as opposed to commercials or nonbroadcast productions.

Tilt: A vertical movement of the camera.

Time-and-a-half: Hours 9 and 10 of a work day, during which time the performer receives 1½ times the hourly rate under most contracts.

Trades: The industry newspapers—*Variety* and *Hollywood Reporter.*

Turnaround: The number of hours between dismissal one day and call time the next day.

Two-Shot: A shot, medium or otherwise, which includes two people. It may be straight on or an **Over-the-Shoulder**.

Typecasting: Casting actors who are physically matched to the characters that are being cast.

Upgrade: To hire a performer in one category, such as extra, and move him or her to a higher category. If an extra player is given a line, she/he is upgraded to principal.

Voice-over (**VO** or **off-screen** or **off-camera**): Off-camera voice work. The voice track produced separately, frequently in a sound studio.

Wardrobe: The clothes that an actor wears in a scene.

Waiver: A document releasing the producer from certain contractual stipulations. Only the union can approve a waiver.

Wardrobe Fitting: A paid session held prior to production to prepare a performer's costumes when the producer is providing costumes.

Whip Pan: A fast, panning movement of the camera.

Wild Lines: Lines that were not scripted, recorded on the set, and built into the track in the dubbing process.

Wild Spot: A commercial which is contracted to air on a station-by-station basis, rather than by network.

"Wrap": A term used when the day's work is completed; "it's a wrap."

Zoom: A camera technique with a special lens to adjust the depth of a shot without moving the camera.